"*Launch Your Encore* is a brief, energizing, life-changing read. The authors, both long-time executives of frontline missions organizations, provide fellow boomers with a sure blueprint for finishing well—as did the original 'Old Dog,' Caleb (his name actually means dog), an octogenarian who led God's people in the capture of Hebron. This book is sure to have a wide appeal and influence because of its broad transcultural principles, compelling personal anecdotes and testimony, clear scriptural basis, and next-step wisdom. Certain to launch many glorious sunsets!"

—**R. Kent Hughes**, senior pastor emeritus,
College Church in Wheaton

"Baby boomers are living longer lives and living healthier lives. Hans and Rick have provided a practical and inspiring guide to help baby boomers live better lives and more fulfilling lives."

—**Dan Bolin**, international director
of Christian Camping International

"An encore means your audience wants more—from *you*. Don't exit your stage—embrace it! *Launch Your Encore* shows you how to engage life's new stages. Warm and practical, this book helps you choose and create realistic expectations for your future. Begin to compose new melodies and write fresh lyrics to your life's song—then present them with all you've got! Inspire your expanding audience to create and perform songs of their own design. There is no 'fine' (ending) to these melodies."

—**Glen Aubrey**, professional musician and publisher,
www.glenaubrey.com

"At seventy-six years of age I can testify that the senior years can be some of the best years and here is a book that can help make it happen. I fear that the people who need this book the most will never even see it, so please get extra copies to give away."

—George Verwer, founder of OM

"A great look into the why and how of energizing our later years with purpose and meaning—with plenty of inspirational, relevant stories and tools for self-assessment and planning."

—Harold Myra, former CEO of Christianity Today International

Launch Your
ENCORE

FINDING ADVENTURE AND PURPOSE
LATER IN LIFE

HANS FINZEL & RICK HICKS

BakerBooks
a division of Baker Publishing Group
Grand Rapids, Michigan

Published by Baker Books
a division of Baker Publishing Group
P.O. Box 6287, Grand Rapids, MI 49516-6287
www.bakerbooks.com

Printed in the United States of America

Library of Congress Cataloging-in-Publication Data is on file at the Library of Congress, Washington, DC.

ISBN 978-0-8010-1686-8

To protect the privacy of those who have shared their stories with the authors, some details and names have been changed.

Published in association with the literary agency of Mark Sweeney & Associates, Bonita Springs, Florida, 34135

In keeping with biblical principles of creation stewardship, Baker Publishing Group advocates the responsible use of our natural resources. As a member of the Green Press Initiative, our company uses recycled paper when possible. The text paper of this book is composed in part of post-consumer waste.

15   16   17   18   19   20   21   7   6   5   4   3   2   1

I, Hans, want to dedicate this book to my wife, Donna. As this book is launched, we are celebrating forty years of marriage. Through all our seasons of life, you have been there by my side. And now, as we are in the middle of launching our encore, it seems more satisfying than ever to walk this path with you. Thank you for your life partnership in the pursuit of all our many dreams.

I, Rick, want to dedicate this book to Kathy, my wife, friend, and "cowriter" in everything I do. We planned our life together, lived it out together, and are now launching our encore together. We are definitely finding adventure and purpose later in our lives.

Contents

Foreword

Our modern terminology clearly implies *retirement* is that golden time of life when we will no longer have to do anything. We will be free from the tyranny of work and will have the luxury of passing the hours in enjoyable leisure. And yet the growing number of baby boomers hitting that magic time of retirement every day do not confirm the thrill of doing nothing. More and more are discovering that "doing nothing" does not provide the enjoyment they expected.

Leo Tolstoy, born into a family of Russian nobility, looked at the lives of his privileged class and the lives of the plain folks who were their laborers. He determined that whatever their hardships, the working folk rested at night in peace and confidence in God's goodness, while those in royalty frequently complained and were unhappy about their lives. He renounced his wealthy class and set out to work in the fields alongside the peasants. He proclaimed that the greatest error of the leisure class was the erroneous belief that "happiness consists in idleness." And as our current day observations are now confirming, Tolstoy concluded we must recognize that work, and not idleness, is an indispensable condition for happiness for every human being.

In my work as a career coach, I am hearing from more and more clients who are intent on finding meaning and purpose in their work, not just at ages twenty-five or forty-five but in their later years as well. People are realizing the emptiness of leaving meaningful work, of withdrawing from making meaningful contributions and of having time with no purposeful activity. Our old understanding of retirement is to "get out of this 'job' and start doing what I really want to do." But as my clients discover and match the best of their talents and passions in work that is fulfilling, purposeful and profitable, the attraction of traditional retirement tends to dissipate.

In *Launch Your Encore*, the authors draw from the premise that "retirement should not be an exit sign, but a door into something fresh, new, and exciting." The authors share their own stories and the choices they have made to remain fully alive. Here are two guys who have looked at the options and have chosen to live with enthusiasm and purpose. Full of inspiring quotations and real-life examples, this book will help you assess where you are and create a plan to continue living fully, rather than dying slowly.

Launch Your Encore gives us the steps to increase our unique contributions to the world as we age, and to continue to live lives rich in love, friendship, and compassion—so we will not be among those referenced by Oliver Wendell Holmes: "Alas for those that never sing, but die with all their music in them."

Dan Miller, *New York Times* bestselling author of
48 Days to the Work You Love (www.48Days.com)

Acknowledgments

We are grateful to our agent, Mark Sweeney of Mark Sweeney & Associates, for his belief in this project and for mentoring us through the journey of getting this material out into the hands of our readers.

A special thank you to Elke Hanssmann for her generous contributions to three of our chapters and lending us her expertise in mentoring and life transitions. (Refer to "About Elke Hanssmann" for more information.)

I, Rick, also want to thank Kathy Hicks for taking my ideas and thoughts and putting them in a form others will understand. I also want to thank Audrey Domeck for typing and retyping many of the original chapters and Lisa Coetzee for her help in some of the early research for this project.

Finally, thank you to the editorial and marketing teams at Baker Publishing Group for their excellent partnership and dedication to delivering this finished product.

Introduction

Bob and Debbie seemed to be a couple who were living what people think is the final act of the American Dream. Bob retired in his early sixties after a successful career in a Fortune 500 company. About the time his retirement came up the company was sold, so he was financially set for life. Bob and Debbie had two wonderful children and two wonderful grandchildren, and had been married for over forty years. They bought a house on the east coast, and for the first decade after Bob's retirement they split their time between their home in California and their home in Virginia. They had plenty of time for their grandchildren and going on cruises to exotic places around the world. Bob had some involvement on a nonprofit board and they attended church.

After ten years of living what Bob thought was his dream, he was feeling increasingly dissatisfied and empty because of the needs he had learned about around the world, needs that he could meet. Recently he had an "Aha!" moment, and said to himself, *Wait a minute, this is not all there is*. He told Hans, "I need to quit doing all this stuff that's *filling my life with fun—but is not fulfilling.* I want to make a difference with the years I have left. I have to make room to make a contribution."

--- --- --- --- ---

On January 1, 2011, baby boomers began turning sixty-five. Between seven and ten thousand of us will celebrate that milestone birthday each day for the next eighteen years. Seventy-six million of us boomers are moving into our sixties and seventies—more than a quarter of the US population. The last wave of boomers turned fifty on January 1, 2014. At every stage of our lives, we have been a national focus for the entertainment industry, the media, and marketers. *Our late-life transition will again rock the world.* By 2050, according to Pew Research projections, about one in five Americans will be over age sixty-five, and about 5 percent will be ages eighty-five and older, up from 2 percent in 2010. These ratios will put the United States at mid-century roughly where Japan, Italy, and Germany—the three "oldest" large countries in the world—are today.[1]

Statistics show that we are living on average twelve years longer than the previous "builder" generation. And in the process we are redefining what is known as "the retirement years." Dr. Laura Carstensen, director of the Stanford Center on Longevity, says, "The culture hasn't had time to catch up. The enormity of this hasn't hit people."[2] We, the authors, are coming to grips with the bonus of these added years, and this book is aimed squarely at helping our aging generation in this transition toward a meaningful and purposeful later life.

As authors, we have pondered our fate approaching this post-career life stage. As a result, we came up with the idea of the "60–80 Window." We have a lot of plans to be productive during our sixties and seventies, and don't plan to retire to a beach or a golf course. Sure, we will do some of that—we have earned it—but we want much more out of these approaching years than the traditional view of retirement. We believe that boomers need to be intentional about finding meaning and purpose in this older stage of life, which brings up a number of key questions. Where will we find significance in the 60–80 Window? How do we find that new place as we leave our main careers? How do we launch a fulfilling encore?

During our journey of writing this book, over a two-year period, we both floated the word *retirement* time and again. We mentioned to strangers and friends alike that we were pioneering new ways of looking at retirement years for boomers who don't really like that "R" word. The comebacks were at times hilarious, chilling, confusing, and enlightening. Most of all, they underscored our observation that for most boomers and younger people there is not much serious thought or preparation for getting ready for this important life transition.

Retirement is many different things for each one of us. One older retired gentleman we ran into said, "My retired friends either love it or hate it." So we asked, "Why do they hate it?" He replied, "Because they have not figured out what to do and they are bored stiff."

Here is just a sampling of other things we heard in our informal survey.

Question: What comes to mind when you hear the word *retirement*?

- My question is, "What's next?"
- Work as long as I can.
- Freedom—finally have time to do what I love.
- I can put off till tomorrow what I don't want to do today.
- I can start over—and do what I will really want to do.

- I can't afford to.
- Retirement is an "employee" concept if you work for yourself.
- Shed my shackles and create a new career.
- I'm finally going to sell this place—all I want is a beach and a beer.
- I don't believe in retirement.
- I will work till I drop dead.

We found some interesting contrasts:

- For some people, "I will love retirement, because I will be free to do what I want. And what I want is fun."
- For others, "I will hate retirement, because my life will no longer have meaning and I will no longer be needed or be important in my career."
- For some people who don't like their jobs, they assume that retirement is more fun than working.
- For other people who love their jobs and their work, they get very depressed at the thought of having to give it up.
- Some people are financially ready for an abundant retirement.
- Other people are scared to death because they are not ready financially to ever stop working though they would love to.

If we had a chance to ask you, how would you fill in this blank? "For me the word retirement means _____."

Getting old is happening to all of us, even to our favorite movie stars. "But I'm kind of comfortable with getting older because it's better than the other option, which is being dead. So I'll take getting older," says George Clooney.[3] That fact being obvious, we want to add that we believe that growing old can be dangerous. The trail is treacherous and the pitfalls are many. One is wise to be prepared. We know it's coming. It's not like God kept the aging process a secret from all of us. It's not like we are blazing a new trail that no one has traveled before. But, like every life stage we have gone through as boomers, from Kennedy's assassination to Woodstock, from Watergate and Vietnam to 9/11 and our two recent wars, it does seem that we are walking "the road less traveled." Why is that? Because, as a generation, we have always thought of ourselves as "different."

Imagine the journey of life like an escalator in your local mall. We get on as infants and start riding up the journey of life. First floor is infancy and childhood. Then we get back on and ride up another floor to land in the stage of adolescence. On up we go, to college and our careers. Probably most of us gather up spouses and children as we keep going up the escalator to new floors. As we ride along, just like at the mall, we can peer down and see what we are leaving behind and look up to see what is coming next. For generations, the final stop on the escalator of life was retirement and death, often in our sixties. But today there is so much more as we stay on the escalator. Today we rise up and reach what we call "the encore floors of *elderlescence*." We view it as a stage of life filled with just as much prominence and adventure as adolescence. Or you might prefer our newly coined phrase that is easier on the tongue, the 60–80 Window. Whatever you want to call it, a whole new floor—or life stage—awaits most of us boomers right now as we move into our sixties and beyond.

Bottom line: *The word* retirement *should not be an exit sign, but a door into something fresh, new, and exciting.* We are in a massive generational changing of the guard, and boomers will redefine the traditional notion of retirement as they reach that top floor in the mall of life. Frankly, retirement is a four-letter word for us, if you listen to most boomers you ask about it. The word smacks of lying on the couch or beach and doing nothing. Dr. Richard Luker, a social psychologist and expert on how Americans spend their leisure time and money, says that this trend of a new view of retirement is dramatically accelerating. "People who are now in their fifties are far more vital in their outlook than people in their fifties were even ten years ago." He goes on to say, "People are saying, 'I'm up for it. I'm game, I want to do more.'"[4]

Most of us do not want to follow the path of our parents, who might have lived long enough to land on the beaches of Florida and drive golf carts. Sure, we want some of that, but along with having more fun and leisure time we also hope to seek meaning and purpose in new, uncharted ways. As we move out of our main-act careers into the encore of our lives, we will most likely want to find roles of influence and purpose that are not based on positions or professions we held in the past but on a lifetime of accumulated experience.

Both of us have a deep passion to mobilize our aging generation for significant impact on the world at this stage of our lives. *We believe that our final act might just be our greatest contribution.* We have earned the right in "retirement" to pursue the joys of golf, grandchildren, cruises, and collecting seashells. But we think that these fun adventures should be coupled with activities and commitments that make a contribution back to society. In the words of Max Lucado, "Your last chapters can be your best. Your final song can be your greatest."[5]

PART 1

The Challenge
More Life after Our Careers

There is a good chance, if you are in your sixties today, that you will make it well into your eighties. I, Hans, just bought some new fifteen-year term life insurance and they assured me I would live well into my eighties and not cash in on the policy before it expires! A whole new life stage is presenting itself to us aging baby boomers as we ponder life beyond our work-a-day careers.

Way back in 1904 G. Stanley Hall observed a change in the demographics of the youth in America. Individuals didn't just go from childhood to adulthood; there seemed to be an emerging stage between the two. He coined a new term and called it *adolescence*. In much the same way, today, we are identifying a new life stage between late adulthood and "old age." Some are calling this stage *elderlescence*; we call it the 60–80 Window. Whatever name is settled on, this is a newly recognized and very dynamic stage of life that needs defining and navigating for those entering into this uncharted phase of life.

Our boomer generation has always seemed to land upon the answers for each season of our lives. But this one is different. As increasing numbers of us are aging, we have disturbing questions about our future that we don't seem to have all the answers for. We are a tidal wave of "children of the 1950s and '60s" who are now turning sixty-plus, and for the first time in our lives we may not have a clear picture of where we are going or how to get there.

"Old age is like everything else. To make a success of it, you've got to start young."[1] So said Theodore Roosevelt. This is good advice for all of us who are hurtling along toward the 60–80 Window years of our lives as boomers.

1 People Get Ready

While working on this book, the two of us were enjoying lunch at a favorite small family restaurant in Colorado. My friend Scott is the owner. He knows that I, Hans, am an author. "So, what are you working on today?" he asked us as we sat with laptops and tablets open. We told him about the new book we were writing about changing the way boomers face retirement. "Oh, I have that all figured out," Scott said. "When I finally sell this place all I want is a beach and a beer." Rick replied, "That might be great for a week or a month, but it won't last." Then Scott, also an aging boomer, offered some deeper insight into his psyche. "You know, our parents' idea of life was totally off the mark. You grow up, get an education, work your whole life for a company, retire, and then you die. That is totally debunked today."

Thanks, Scott. That is exactly our point. The fact is, we have a lot of life left on the escalator after our careers are over. Scott was the perfect setup for our message. He knows that what his parents thought about retirement no longer stacks up, but he seems very fuzzy about what the new reality is all about and he does not seem prepared for it. Scott will soon learn that there is a whole lot more to living in our 60–80 Window than a beach and a beer and some golf and grandkids. *Yes*, whatever you love you should continue to enjoy doing at this life stage—but we would argue that there is a whole lot more, beyond leisure.

Have you ever wished you could tell the future? Wouldn't it be great to know what's coming next in life? You wouldn't be surprised by what happens to you, and you would always be prepared for things that are coming your way. In a way, that's how I, Rick, spent much of my adult life. I didn't exactly know the future but I did have a good idea of what types of things were going to happen next in my life. I've been studying life stage development since I was in my late twenties, and ended up getting my PhD, focusing on developmental psychology. When I was in my thirties I knew what was coming in my forties. For instance, most people need to start using reading glasses in their forties, and if we expect that it is easier to accept and adjust when the time comes.

In my forties I knew what to expect in my fifties. One of those eventualities is diminishing physical strength. I remember the "Aha!" moment when I was about fifty-five and visiting our OM (Operation Mobilization) ship with a heavy backpack and overpacked suitcase. I had rolled the suitcase from where I had been dropped off, along the quayside, to the bottom of the gangplank of the ship. A young man in his twenties stepped forward and offered to carry my suitcase up the gangplank for me. My first reaction was to think, *I don't need this kid to carry my suitcase. I am perfectly capable.* But when I went to pick it up, I realized how heavy it really was and that I would have a hard time carrying it up. So I had to give in to the fact that I wasn't as strong as I used to be and let the young man help me. Knowing that diminishing strength is typical of people in their fifties made it easier to accept. I didn't like it, but I had to accept it.

While in my fifties, looking forward to my sixties, I was surprised to find that there wasn't much information out there about this next stage. It seems that most mainstream research on life stage development stops when it reaches late adulthood. The more I searched for information on this stage of life the more I realized that the years from sixty to eighty have not been studied as thoroughly as the earlier stages. This left me a little disappointed in terms of anticipating what developmental tasks I would be dealing with in my sixties.

All of my adult life I have looked forward to the next stage of life and had some notions of what would be coming my way. I think this gave me a distinct advantage over others who seemed surprised at how life continually changes. I wanted to have that same advantage and be able to anticipate what's coming in the next few decades—so that started me on a research quest to identify this new, emerging stage of life. Hans and I want to share the findings with you to give you the same advantage.

Unless you are living under a rock, you have no doubt observed that a massive new life stage has appeared. In the past people tended to retire at age sixty-five and die soon thereafter. Now people aren't necessarily dying at sixty-eight or seventy-eight or even eighty-eight. More people are living longer due to healthier lifestyles and medical advances. So now we have a new life stage from the midsixties to the mideighties and beyond, creating the need for people to figure out what to do with their lives. We're glad to be able to share our discoveries with you! We want to help our generation of boomers "land" on great ideas that will make all of our lives during this 60–80 Window more *meaningful* and *productive*.

Life Stage Development for Dummies

Remember the escalator analogy of life in our introduction? Well, consider each floor at that mall of life as a life stage. A quick overview of "life stage development" will help you understand what these different stages are and how significantly they impact our day-to-day lives. When you think about it, the concept of life stages is not that unique or uncommon. We see examples of it in nature all around us. Think about salmon. They go through stages in a similar way as humans do. They are hatched from eggs and become "fry," and then grow into "smelt." Then they make their way downstream and feed and grow in the ocean. After a few years they head back to their streams and spawn, preparing to produce eggs for the cycle to start all over again.

In each of these stages there are tasks that need to be accomplished to get them ready for the next stage: from hatching, to growing into smelt (when they are transformed in a way that makes it possible for them to live in salt water), to migrating, to strengthening themselves during ocean life, and then finally to making the difficult swim back upstream to spawn. They all follow the same stages to live out their life cycle.

Our lives are like that, in a way. We grow, develop, and change one stage at a time. But our stages are not driven by mere instinct. They are driven by moral and behavioral choices, which help to develop our personality. Therefore, life stages are a blueprint of the issues and areas of life we need to deal with and the general order in which they tend to come.

Erik Erikson is probably the best-known theorist on life stage development. Many of us studied his theories in our Psych 101 class in college. Erikson lists eight stages and what tasks need to be accomplished in each stage.

In the following chart you can see that each stage has two opposing emotional forces. The developmental task in each stage is to achieve a healthy balance between these opposing dispositions.

Erickson's Eight Psychosocial Stages[1]

Psychosocial Crisis Stage	Life Stage	Age Range/Other Descriptions
1. Trust vs. Mistrust	Infancy	0–1½ years, baby, birth to walking
2. Autonomy vs. Shame and Doubt	Early childhood	1–3 years, toddler, toilet training
3. Initiative vs. Guilt	Play age	3–6 years, preschool, nursery
4. Industry vs. Inferiority	School age	5–12 years, early school
5. Identity vs. Role Confusion	Adolescence	9–18 years, puberty, teens
6. Intimacy vs. Isolation	Young adulthood	18–40 years, courting, early parenthood
7. Generativity vs. Stagnation	Adulthood	30–65 years, middle age, parenting
8. Integrity vs. Despair	Mature age	50+ years, old age, grandparents

Each stage in life becomes a bit more complex and is rooted in the previous stage. As we move along in life, there are continual developmental stages to work on to enable us to grow to our full potential. Erikson focused on the younger years and, as was stated earlier, not as much on the late adult years. You can see for yourself the glaring omission of the 60–80 Window from his chart.

After Erikson, Daniel Levinson came along and focused on adult male development (in a later work he expanded his research to include women). In referring to the various seasons of a man's life Levinson states, "The life structure evolves through a relatively orderly sequence during the adult years. . . . It consists of a series of alternating stable (structure-building) periods and transitional (structure-changing periods.)"[2]

Developmental Periods in the Eras of Early and Middle Adulthood

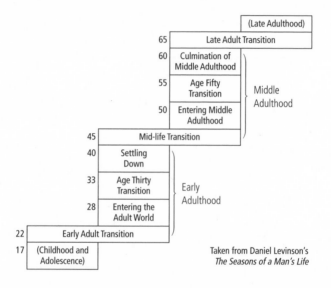

What does all this mean for you and me? As adults, we continue to grow and develop in different stages of life whether we are conscious of it or not. In this book, we are addressing the "late adult transition" time of life. It can be a scary time because we are entering uncharted territory and there is no more time for the "do-overs" that were possible in our younger years.

As you look at this last chart, it is helpful to know that our lives tend to alternate between transition and stable life stages.

If we are aware of what developmental tasks are associated with each stage, we can be prepared for some of the normal changes of life that are coming. (For a fuller description of what these tasks are, see our reading list in the Resources section and also www.launchyourencore.com.)

When considering life stages, I, Rick, find it is easier to boil it down to what was described to me by Ray Rood, one of my professors in graduate school, as a tribal view of life development.[3]

A Tribal View of Life Development

Aged
Minimal purpose

Elder
Imparting wisdom

Journeyman
Worker/Leader

Apprentice
Learning from community

Child
Learning from family

This is a more concise view of the divisions of our lives. It is not as complicated as the other models and gets right to the point. As a child and apprentice, we continue to learn from family and others in society. As a journeyman, we take our adult positions in life, whatever that is for us. Whether we are a businessperson, firefighter, teacher, or homemaker, we are assuming our main act on the stage of life. We are fulfilling our adult position in society for many decades, lasting usually from our thirties well into our sixties.

After our main journeyman years comes this stage we call *elders*. Maybe that word turns you off because you don't feel qualified. "Me? An elder?" It does sound old . . . and responsible, but that is what we face next. There is a major shift in our place in society as we move to a position in which we share the wisdom we have learned over our lifetime. Have you noticed how many people start calling you "sir" or "ma'am"? Maybe you don't feel like you have a lot of wisdom to share. Whether you have grasped it or not, we in the 60–80 Window do have lessons on life to share with others. These lessons are the takeaways we have learned. They've grown out of a long life of successes and failures. We'll unpack how and where we can share this wisdom much more in later chapters.

Whether you resonate most with Erikson, Levinson, or the tribal view, *the point remains that different things are expected of us at different stages of our lives*. The more we know about what might be taking place in our future, the better prepared we are at finding meaning and purpose at each stage of life, including these later years.

We both find the concept of the elder stage to be particularly meaningful for us right now. As we are stepping out of organizational leadership roles, we are experiencing the satisfaction of not being in charge of everything, and of being able to share lessons in life we have learned over the years. We are in the process of becoming men of wisdom as we find opportunities to share our successes and failures with others.

Here is a recent experience that illustrates this, one that actually took place in a remote village in Africa. I, Rick, learned that you don't have to be in a position of leadership to be in a place of great influence. A group of us were asked to visit a remote fishing village in Zambia. I wasn't the leader of the group. I had been the leader of this visiting organization for several years, but a couple of years earlier had turned over the leadership to a younger man, Andrew, whom I had been mentoring for a number of years. He was leading this group, but I was along to visit the work of our local team there and participate in the work they were doing in this small village.

I had been helping fit reading glasses to the villagers, but was abruptly called to meet with the "headman," the chief elder of the village. As the oldest man in our group, I was perceived as the elder and the one who could share wisdom and advice, even though technically Andrew had more authority. The village elder shared with me his two most pressing problems and asked if I could give him advice. They were overwhelming issues and I didn't have the specific solutions for his problems, but I was able to give him advice on a way forward.

As I was talking with the headman I realized that I didn't necessarily have to have all of the answers. I could draw from my own experiences, even my failures, in ways that could be helpful in advising him. After I gave him what I thought would be helpful advice, it occurred to me that I might be having more of an impact on people as an elder/advice-giver than as the president of my organization.

Both of us authors are right in the middle of this journey of transition from positional influence to life impact. As we continue the ride up our escalator to later life, we are *laying aside positions of authority and taking up places of influence.* This is a new stage of life for us, and one that is taking time to adjust to. We miss the adrenaline of being in the center of all the action from our main careers, but we are finding it can be even more fulfilling to be in this new place of elder impact. As the song said so well, "People get ready, there's a train a-comin'. You don't need no baggage, you just get on board."[4] We all need to learn how to get on that train and not to be run over by it! And . . . we hope to give you some good baggage to take along for the trip to make it as successful as possible.

2   I Can't Get No Respect

Every time we mention the two words *Social Security* to our young adult children, their temperatures rise and they get that "I am so angry at the government" look on their faces. "You have it made, Dad; it will be there for you. And we will be paying for you and all your boomer buddies for the rest of our lives. But there will be *nothing* left for us when we get old."

We boomers at every stage have been described as a "pig passing through a python," making our whims and desires a national focus. The economy caters to our needs at every stage, from Beetles to Beemers. We are the generation still on the center stage in our society, leading, from the younger set still in their fifties such as Stephen Colbert, Barack Obama, and Jeff Bezos to the older gang made up of the likes of Ron Howard, Hillary Clinton, Rush Limbaugh, and Cher.

As we age, interesting generational conflicts will be on the rise as never before. The very mass of our size in society is a setup for conflict. For now there seems to be a growing tension in this country between the nation's rapidly growing aging population and the younger population that someday will be responsible for the mental, emotional, and financial well-being of the boomers. What we observe about the American scene is being played out, as well, in many other countries with very similar demographics. China, for example, has recently reversed their one child policy for the very reason that they have hundreds of millions of boomers who will need to be cared for in their elder years by their children and grandchildren.

As we are writing this chapter Jay Leno is being forced to retire from the *Tonight Show* at age sixty-three, and young Jimmy Fallon is replacing him. By the time you read this who knows what will have happened. Jay wanted to do one network interview about his departure, so he called in his friend Steve Croft from *60 Minutes*, who had interviewed Jay when he took over the show from Johnny Carson twenty-two years earlier. The interview of Jay Leno by Steve Croft for *60 Minutes* was telling. Steve was echoing our message. He mentioned that we all are in the giant "generational changing of the guard," a term we as authors have been using for years. Boomers have to move aside, and everywhere they are being forced out and replaced with the younger generations whether they like it or not. It was very clear in the interview that Jay did not want to quit the *Tonight Show*. And to his credit, it actually led late-night television ratings for most of the years he was on. NBC forced Jay Leno out while he was consistently number one in the ratings . . . because the time for boomers is over for many people.

Whether we boomers like it or not, there is a pressure for us to move aside. Jay Leno's challenge became, "What do I do next?" To his credit he was being positive and not whining about the inevitable, a lesson for all of us. We can get all tied up in our shorts and fight it with anger and bitterness, or we can accept this generational changing of the guard and find our next encore act. Jay chose the latter, and that is a good example for all of us. Of course he does have the advantage of millions stashed away, which makes for a very soft landing!

Some of us in our aging years have the power to decide our fates, but many of us don't. All of us need to recognize the reality that this generational conflict is real and is getting more intense. How can we turn it in our favor and be ahead of the wave? An illustration of the tension and shortsightedness of younger generations toward their elders is found in an old Balinese legend.

It is said that once upon a time the people of a remote mountain village used to sacrifice and eat their old men. The day came when there was not a single old man left and the traditions were lost. They wanted to build a great house for the meeting of the assembly, but when they came to look at the tree trunks that had been cut for that purpose, no one could tell the top from the bottom. If the timbers were placed the wrong way up, it would set off a series of disasters. A young man said if they would promise never to eat the old men anymore, he would be able to find a solution. They promised. He brought his grandfather whom he had hidden and the old man taught the community to tell the top from the bottom.[1]

In much the same way, in American society today, we ostracize the elderly without any consideration for what we lose when we don't keep them as a part of our active community. Many other cultures around the world respect and honor the elderly of their society for the wisdom, maturity, and experience they have gained over their lifetime. In those cultures, the young want to tap into what the elders have to offer them. But it's clearly evident in our Western society that this respect and honor have disappeared. If this issue isn't addressed, our society will lose so much of the experience and acquired knowledge that the elder generation has.

There are those among the younger generations who really have it out for the boomers. Take, for example, an article written by Janine White, a Generation X woman, that was published in *Philadelphia Magazine*, March 2011. After mentioning the statistic that starting January 1, 2011, seven thousand to ten thousand baby boomers a day started turning sixty-five, and would continue to do so for eighteen years, she expressed her frustration:

> I don't know when this never-ending story—essentially the story of boomers getting old—started dominating our news, politics and culture. For me, a smack-in-the-middle-of-Generation-X adult of 38 years, the interminable aging process of this massive generation has always been there, casting a shadow over my future like, well, a parasite ready to suck the life out of my highest-earning-potential years. That it has arrived in the midst of a bad recession just seems to be the icing on the tapeworm. Boomers may finally be queuing for their long-stretching shuffle off into the sunset, but they're still a large majority in power and still controlling the national conversation.[2]

Ouch. That was a bit harsh. But we have both run into people in the younger generations who are this amped up about the issue of boomer dominance. We don't know about you other boomers, but for us it does not seem that we boomers are still controlling the national conversation. Just dip into Facebook, Twitter, Pinterest, LinkedIn, the blog world, and the rest of social media, and you see where the young are leading the national conversation. In fact, more boomers every day are feeling left out of that growing online conversation by the sheer reality that social media and the almost daily changes therein are a foreign country to many who are living in the 60–80 Window stage of life.

On the flipside of this generational coin, we've observed that many boomers' views of the younger generations also have a lack of respect toward the youth of today. This counter-reaction from the boomer camp shows how many aging boomers are not all that fond of their children's generation and can get downright judgmental:

> As a baby boomer, I can freely note that part of the problem with the younger generation is that someone forgot to teach many of them respect for their elders! No one gets out of this alive, and I recall a time when elders were valued for the wisdom of a long life well lived. Technology, while I enjoy it, has come to replace true, heartfelt, sincere communication. Wisdom from having "Googled" does not replace wisdom from having lived![3]

We would love to see this apparent "great divide" bridged between the younger generations and us boomers, and we have discovered facts that can help and hopefully can clarify to our kids' generations the great value boomers add to our American society.

Rob Romasco, as president of AARP, answered three critical myths in a brief article:

Myth #1: *Older people are a drain on the economy, leaving the next generation with less.* What is the real truth? People over fifty bolster our US economy to the tune of seven trillion a year; and that is expected to double by 2032. Plus, the taxes paid by those over fifty make up half of all the tax revenue of the US, state, and local governments.

Myth #2: *Social Security and Medicare benefit only older Americans.* What is the real truth? One in every five beneficiaries of Social Security is under sixty-five, including 4.4 million children. Social Security death and disability benefits are a huge lifeline to millions of younger Americans and their families. And most people feel that these two crucial safety nets will be fixed in the next two decades when the national conversation gets strong enough.

Myth #3: *The young and old are rival armies in a struggle over finite resources, and the old are winning.* What is the real truth? One day the young of today will be the old of tomorrow. We are all at different places on our life journey. Today the older help the younger, and tomorrow the roles will be reversed. The two should be partners in life's journey, not rivals.[4]

We, the authors, are both optimists and idealists. Both sides of the great generational divide should reach out to the other. Our hope and dream is that the two sides of this divide can indeed come together and appreciate each other's role in our society today. The most balanced and healthy society and church has a place for all generations. We believe that is the way God designed it.

3 Transition Is Unavoidable

I, Rick, found myself in the jungles of South America teaching a leadership course to a group of ex-patriots who were gathered to work on their master's degree in leadership development. These people couldn't take time away from their work to come to the States to obtain their degree, so the professors were sent to them. I taught my course on leadership in the afternoons and one of my colleagues taught a morning course on dealing with transitions. Having nothing else to do in the jungle, I sat in on her class and it changed my life.

I had recently experienced a transition that involved leaving one job and starting another. I had hired a good number of people at Biola University, the place I was leaving, and didn't want to particularly say goodbye or make a big deal out of my departure. So, instead of bringing closure, I just told people, "I'm not really leaving; I'm just moving to a job not far from here. We will still be friends and continue our relationships."

I left my work on Friday, we moved on Saturday and got situated in our new house on Sunday, and I started my new job on Monday. I didn't leave a lot of time for transition—no thought process or room for feelings. I was a few months into the new job when I was asked to teach this course in the jungles of South America, and that's when I stumbled onto these principles of transition. It helped me realize that I had never really processed my departure. I had just put it off, denied it, and stuffed it down in myself without dealing with it. After becoming aware of what is involved in a proper transition, I realized that I needed to go back and say goodbye to the people I had previously worked with.

The principles of transition can best be learned from William Bridges in his defining book, *Transitions*. He describes three phases during transition: *endings*, the first phase, as you can't start a new beginning until you end your previous situation; the *neutral zone*, the middle phase, as once you have declared your ending you need to take some time, sit back, think, and process what it is that you are no longer a part of or what new situation you are embarking on, which may be the loss of a loved one, the loss of a job, a new home, a new spouse, a new child in the family, or any one of a myriad of transitions that we go through; and the *new beginning*, the final phase of the transition, as you can't start a new beginning until you have completed the ending and started the neutral zone. If you start the new beginning anywhere else it short-circuits the process. That is clearly what I experienced.[1]

After I became aware of this, four months later I went back to my colleagues at Biola and began to actually say goodbye. One of the key people with whom I had worked sat across the desk from me and said, "I wondered if you were ever going to come back and bring any closure." At that point she began to tear up, and then I did as well. It was clear to me that I had all these emotions deep down inside I hadn't acknowledged or let go of. I had never intentionally ended my time at Biola.

Others around me, who were more sensitive to the situation, were quite aware of what was happening. This was really an epiphany for me. I needed to end what I had done at Biola before I could fully engage in my new job.

This story happened back in the early eighties. Since then I've read about this process, studied it, and even taught it in a number of seminars. But it happened to me again just a few weeks ago. I was in the process of moving back to California after living in Atlanta for seventeen years. My job wasn't changing. I just no longer needed to live in Atlanta to fulfill my responsibilities. As people were trying to say goodbye to me, I would tell them, "I'll still be back here in the office four or five times a year, so we don't need to say goodbye."

Then, just as I was about to address my co-workers at a send-off luncheon they held for me and my wife, Kathy, it struck me. I was doing the same thing I had done almost three decades ago. I was not owning up to what was really happening to me. I didn't want to admit that I was really leaving. The pain of saying goodbye was something I was trying to avoid.

Transitions continue to happen in our lives, and the same principles apply. I can tell you that this time the transition went smoother because I did face the pain of saying goodbye. I did acknowledge that my relationships would look, feel, and, in fact, be different. If we follow the principles of the transition process, it makes it easier on ourselves and on those around us.

Transitions are an important part of all stages of life development. But they are particularly treacherous in our elder years because we often don't have a chance for do-overs. At this later stage of our lives, there are so many things that we are transitioning through it can be dizzying! We are facing major changes relating to our jobs, health, family, and finances. One major fact for boomers, who are often called the "sandwich generation," is that we are dealing with so many major life changes at the same time. The empty nest, the weddings of our kids, the births of grandkids, our own aging, and helping our elderly and dying parents. We need to be aware of how great the impact of these life transitions truly is as we consider where we have been and where we are going.

Sometimes the shock of these transitions arrive on the same day! For me, Hans, and my wife, Donna, that was our reality in one twenty-four-hour period! The dates were January 7 and 8, 2013. We were celebrating Christmas late, because that was when all twelve of our family could be here in Denver, "under our roof." They all came into town to be present for my farewell dinner, which was being held by our ministry, WorldVenture, on the evening of January 8 and which marked the end of my twenty years as president as well as the end of thirty-two total years of belonging to the family of WorldVenture that both Donna and I had given the bulk of our careers and lives to.

On January 7, during our Christmas gift exchange time, we had a blast opening gifts and watching our grandkids open theirs and play. Then we all received the exciting and surprising news from our son, Jeremy, and daughter-in-law, Jordan, that she was expecting baby number two. What great joy we all had as big brother Nicholas told us, while pointing at his mommy's tummy, "There's a baby in there!" Talk about a high! It doesn't get much better than that.

Donna and the family had prepared a big Christmas dinner for that evening. Just as we were finishing eating our meal, Donna got an urgent call from her sister that her mom, Anita, was dying. Despite the long battle Anita had endured with

Alzheimer's disease, the end actually came very suddenly, and in just about twelve hours, at 2:00 a.m. on January 8, she died. Donna was unable to rush to her father's side in Phoenix because of all the family and events, and the shock of these dramatic, polar-opposite life events hit her, and all of us, hard!

On the morning of the 8th, Donna was encircled by all "the girls" while preparing a family favorite meal for brunch. They were all trying to console Donna, who had now just lost her mother. Even little two-year-old Ireland, the only granddaughter at the time, just wanted to sit on "Nama's" lap as the tears flowed freely. Having all our family present, with their love, hugs, prayers, and comfort in her time of grief, was a great gift from God for Donna. Talk about the circle of life!

In some ways, we weren't able to even take in the magnitude of such a twenty-four-hour period. Later on that evening we all prepared to go to the farewell dinner, where we had to perk up and enjoy a very special evening. It was a beautifully prepared program honoring my tenure as president as well as both of us and our years of leadership with WorldVenture. Surrounded by our family, many of our closest friends, and former colleagues, that momentous day was bittersweet, indeed. Wow, what an impact we experienced during those few days! New life, death, and career end all in one day's time.

If we acknowledge reality, we admit transition is unavoidable. We need to become the elders of our tribe, but that does not happen automatically. Both of us see the issue of denial as one of the greatest dangers we face at this stage of life. Denial that we are in for huge changes as it comes to our role in society and our perceived self-worth. Denial that we are getting older and that people view us differently. There are many dangers of denial as we move into our 60–80 Window.

We have already made it clear that our generation hates the word *retirement*. Yet it is happening to us whether we like it or not! People are asking us more frequently, "Are you retired yet?" or "How are you liking retirement?" For those of us who have gone through it, there is a certain pain to having that retirement party and turning over our keys. After I, Hans, had that party given in my honor, I rode off into the sunset and left behind a thirty-two-year career with one organization. *I was so ready to go, but not at all prepared for what came next.*

I had been the CEO of a multinational nonprofit for twenty years. For all the pressures and headaches of that kind of position, it was satisfying to be so needed and at the center of everything. I loved having people lined up at my door to see me, the phone ringing off the hook, constant invitations to travel, and new email in an inbox that was already overwhelmed. After being "in the game" for so long, all of a sudden I was left to sit in the bleachers. I experienced the pain of leaving my position in my career that gave me so much of my identity, meaning, value, and influence. It was my decision to retire early, but that does not lessen the impact of life after the fast lane. I moved out of my beautiful office. The line stopped. The emails dried up. The invitations evaporated . . . as I faded into the sunset.

What happens to our self-identities when we face the necessary endings of our careers? Most of us have to face an overhaul. Some make it work and some don't. What happens to us after we leave our jobs or the major roles we played in life? When we say goodbye, will our phones ever ring again? Will our email inboxes be filled only with junk mail? Will anybody other than our grandchildren want to relate to us? How will we fill the new space that these endings opened up? We may very well find ourselves battling feelings of worthlessness.

When our identities have been based on our roles or our jobs, it can become a huge identity issue. I, Hans, certainly struggled with those feelings all of my first year away from my high-octane career.

Here is some good news we want to share with you. We want to introduce you to this new stage of life called elderlescence, which can be a very positive experience. This word is so new that most dictionaries don't have it yet. It is the period of life, or life stage, between one's career and traditional old age. As we get older in years, we can leverage our wisdom even more than in our previous positions, and have a great impact in this elderlescence stage. We see that for many of us, this greater impact will be during the 60–80 Window. The possibilities are endless to pick up new roles through such things as doing community service, volunteering, finding a new-stage-of-life career, mentoring, doing ministry in our churches, and a host of other options.

As we all transition toward the 60–80 Window, the key is to know that things will be different. Let's step into this underexplored time of life with hope and expectation. Yes, we have gone from being the youth to the adults, and now we're the elders among those around us. That opens, for all of us, a world of potential where we can find greatly fulfilling and sorely needed roles in our society and around the world.

The book *Counseling Adults in Transition* highlights factors that help transitions be successful. Some of these might serve as additional pointers for us:

- Transitions that are made by choice rather than imposed are much easier to navigate.
- People who have built a good support team as they undergo major transitions are more likely to succeed.

- All of us have previously utilized change and transition strategies that we can re-activate—it is worth thinking about how we dealt with major changes before.
- In times of transition we all need islands of stability—things that do not change.[2]

Beware of Going to the Dark Side

4

Bernard Baruch, on his eighty-fifth birthday, observed that, "To me, old age is always fifteen years older than I am."[1] That rings very true for both of us. No one looks forward to old age even though we don't want to die either. And so, we've got good news and bad news about your future. The good news is that you have a lot of great options out there if you choose them. The bad news is that if you live in denial and drift along, you might just find yourself in a dark place after your career is over. You may get to a place where you feel very old because of choices you have avoided.

You probably know some people who are having the time of their lives in their "retirement" years. We do. They seem to have it all together. And perhaps you have also watched some people close to you struggle and go into a place of despair and darkness in the retirement years because they were not prepared and made bad choices. We see some of our elderly parents thrive while others struggle in their sunset years. Our personal quest is to go to the good place, that place of fulfillment, contribution, and joy in our encore during our sixties, seventies, and even eighties.

Just today I, Hans, took my good friend Jeanelle, who is ninety-six years old, out to lunch in Long Beach, California. We used to live there years ago, and every chance I have when I am back there I try to see her for a meal. (OK, to be accurate, she never lets me pay if we go out, which we always do.) Jeanelle is an amazing example of a bright, positive spirit who has aged the way I want to. When I picked her up in my rental car, she was waiting at the door of her condo building with her walker and a huge grin on her face. In all these years she has never been gloomy or depressed when I picked her up.

So today I decided to ask Jeanelle, "Why are you always so bright, positive, and cheerful? And funny!" She has a lot she could gripe about. She buried two husbands and never had children of her own. She grew up in the Depression when life was tough in America. But she told me that her dad was a negative person and her mother was always positive, so she decided early on to side with her mother. So then I drilled a bit deeper, asking her the key to her happiness in her sunset years. "I make sure I have a lot of friends a lot younger than me, like you, Hans," she said. "Secondly, I make myself get up, dressed, and out the door as much as possible, with a social life." Jeanelle told me she has a lady who shows up every morning at 8:15 to help her get dressed, and it takes an hour. "Many people when they get older just quit trying. They stay inside and wither and die," she said.

So her two keys to longevity are to have friends who are younger and to keep that social life going. Because all of her friends her age are gone! And then I realized that the reason younger people like to be friends with Jeanelle is that she is positive, outgoing, and funny. Here is an example of what she told me today: "When I met with my new estate planner ten years ago, he asked me what happened to my two husbands. With a straight face I told him that I shot them both," she said, with a twinkle in her eyes. Jeanelle has had a lot of heartache, but you would never see her turn that into a pity party. She never goes anywhere near the dark side.

We have choices to make. We have issues to consider. Going to the light equals a positive, productive, and engaging lifestyle. The dark side focuses on a negative, declining, and diminishing outlook on life. Obviously we need to avoid this dark place if at all possible.

Even the mighty King David in the Bible slipped into the dark side in his later years. He lamented in Psalm 31:12, "I am forgotten as though I were dead." That is just the way we can feel when marginalized in our later years. With all his grand accomplishments as warrior, poet, and king, David was quickly set aside as irrelevant by those he so faithfully served all his life. A man as powerful as him wrestled with great negative emotions in his old age as he slipped to the dark side. Charles Spurgeon, one of the greatest writers about the Bible in the 1800s, observed in his *Treasury of David*:

> All David's youthful prowess was now gone from remembrance; he had been the saviour of his country, but his services were buried in oblivion. Men soon forget the deepest obligations; popularity is evanescent to the last degree: he who is in every one's mouth today may be forgotten by all tomorrow.[2]

No one is immune from this later-in-life battle—known by everyone today, forgotten tomorrow.

We've had to make choices about our personal well-being all of our lives. Every developmental stage brought new things to learn and new choices to make. But who would have ever thought, in the elder stage of our life, that we would have to make drastic choices once again? The good news about our elderlescence is that we do have choices. A big part of the choice is to decide: Do we remain the same as we were in our previous stages, or do we make adjustments for our changing life situations in the areas of our finances, health, emotions, and even employment?

Let's explore the idea of self-worth. It becomes a huge struggle for many of us after our main-act careers. Like it or not, we who live in Western cultures live in the reality that "doing" is more important than "being." We judge one another by our jobs and careers and education and what we accomplish and how much we accumulate. We try to keep up with the "Joneses" next door, even though we might not even like them!

So when it comes to later life, when that career is over, where is our self-worth now? The worst thing we can do as we grow older is to wallow in great memories of what we were in the past. The past might have been great, but we cannot live there. I, Hans, look back on my career with great satisfaction for what I accomplished. But I also have to realize that it is over, like a morning fog that lifted and is gone. In his book *Aging: The Fulfillment of Life*, Henri Nouwen says, "There can hardly be a more alienating feeling than that which believes, 'I am who I was.'" He goes on to observe, "Old age is the last segregation. This seems a very appropriate expression in a civilization in which, 'being' is, in fact, considered less important than 'doing' and 'having.'"[3]

Sadly, many forces in our society push us toward that lonely dark side as we age and the "doing" slows down.

The question in later life is not, "Who was I?" It really needs to be, "Who am I now becoming?" Nouwen is right. We need to get beyond what we were and embrace the future as we move forward to what we can become for this great elder stage in life. Now back to that good news, bad news scenario. Henri Nouwen goes on in his book on aging to lay out the choices we have. On the one hand, as we get older, we can move to the dark side—be a little negative, be a little pessimistic, feel bitter about how life has ended up, and actually feel entitled. Much of the research shows that when we take this more negative stance it has an adverse impact on our emotional and physical well-being.

We have all known people who have lived a healthy, productive, and fulfilling life. But as the years pass and old age creeps up, circumstances change and options diminish. The next thing that happens is withdrawal from friends, family, and community. This withdrawal is the first stage of going to the dark side. Pretty soon this person seldom leaves their house and signs of depression set in. A bad mental outlook leads to bitterness and a sense of entitlement. As a result, they don't enjoy being around others and others don't enjoy their company. The final stage of this dark place takes a huge toll physically and mentally on the person, and all too often the story ends with a premature death.

On the other hand, we can choose to be more positive and move to the light—be an encouragement, reflect on what life has given us and pass that on to others, and contribute to society. We make the changes necessary to avoid that dark place at all costs. This can lead to more meaning and purpose as we age. Let's use people like Jeanelle as our role models for this next stage.

Obtaining this more positive outlook on life may require that we re-invent ourselves. That means looking beyond who we *were* and embracing who we can *become*. Some people have the luxury of dipping in and out of retirement, like Tom the firefighter, whom we will meet in chapter 13. But for most of us, we will have to find some new paths.

I, Rick, remember having to forge a new path in my career a few years back. I was given a promotion that included a broader span of authority, more autonomy, and more relationships with a wider spectrum of people. It was a promotion but it was also a transition out of command and control to becoming more of an advisor, a transition many of us will face later in life. The way I had done my previous job just didn't work well in this new role. I didn't make the transition well and I kept trying to do the new job in the old way. It occurred to me at one point that if I didn't change my outlook, if I didn't approach this differently, I was never going to succeed at what I was doing. Once I acknowledged that I had a new role and new responsibilities and needed new ways of doing things, it made it much easier for me to meet the new expectations that were placed upon me. I was free to do things differently without feeling guilty.

I learned that I couldn't do things the same old way and expect different outcomes. We have all heard that the definition of insanity is to "do things the same way but expect different results." I needed to reinvent myself. I needed to consider what the new situation was and what was needed to match up to that. This will be a common experience for all of us who move from one career to the next in later life. Reinvention is the name of the game!

As we move into the elder stage of life, change is certainly more difficult. Reinventing ourselves will not come as easily as it once did. But if we know this is coming, then the mandate for change may not be as difficult. This is something we can actually prepare for in order to avoid the dark side.

In one sense we are standing on the shore with a warning to you, our readers. Our desire is that you will make the right choices to "move toward the light" by taking action now to launch your own encore. We will help prepare you with information and application. Don't drift into the darkness of indifference or despair. You have so much to contribute to your world, and now is the time to start.

5 Elderlescence

Not long ago I, Rick, had an extra day off from work due me, and because my wife was at work, I stayed home, vegged out on the couch, and watched daytime television for hours.

The ratio of commercials to actual television programming is amazing. There must have been a lot of older people watching television at that time of day because many of the commercials were aimed at us. These commercials don't make us look too bright or durable. There are commercials about falling and not getting up, removing brown spots from our skin, and women having leaky pipes. It seems that men's pipes don't leak as much. We also apparently don't know how to invest our money and so we should put it all in gold. If that doesn't work, we can get a reverse home mortgage just to survive. After a day of watching all that I was ready to go back to work and deny that I was getting older!

Although we can't deny our age, and even if some of the old parts don't work as well or look as good as they used to, we do have some reasons to embrace who we are at this older

51

age. One of my favorite shirts is my "OLD GUYS RULE" T-shirt. Wherever I wear it I get a laugh, a chuckle, or a word of encouragement.

Most people really do understand that no matter how old we are getting, and no matter how much we may have forgotten, we still have a lifetime of acquired wisdom and understanding of how life works. It is something to embrace and something we can share with the younger generations. That is pretty much the core of the idea of elderlescence.

We are living longer and staying healthier than any previous generation. And with that time and energy we have a lot to give and a lot to do. Even AARP is getting in on the elderlescence bandwagon with their new "Life Reimagined" initiative. They too are tossing the old "retire at sixty-five and go to the beach" paradigm in favor of helping people who will live a lot longer find meaning and purpose and reimagine their lives at this stage.

> Boomers and older Americans are giving retirement a major makeover: The old stereotype of the 65-year-old trotting off to a sun-filled life of leisure is quickly becoming a thing of the past. A new life stage is emerging—one that takes place between leaving a career in one field and flat-out retiring. Think of it as an "encore career."[1]

Think encore, not pasture. You may think that you don't have much wisdom to share. One perspective is that you can share with others the various mistakes and pitfalls you have encountered and the lessons you learned through them. We can help those who come after us not make the same mistakes we've made. That can be a career in itself!

You don't have to be an expert on a subject to share some age-acquired wisdom. It may simply be drawing on a life lesson from your past. I remember when Kathy and I were driving out to Palm Springs to celebrate our first wedding anniversary (that's forty years ago now). It was about 120 degrees in the desert and our old clunker car started to overheat. I pulled off to the side of the road and took a look at my steaming engine. I didn't know what I was doing, but I thought if I loosened the radiator cap, it would relieve the steaming pressure. Well, it did! Hot pressurized steam boiled out of the radiator and burnt my left arm. Not a great way to start your anniversary weekend! Fast-forward forty years: a younger friend drove into my driveway with his car steaming and overheating. He opened the hood and reached for the radiator cap to loosen it. Looking down at my left arm and feeling the pain from forty years ago, I said, "I'm not a mechanic, and I don't know a lot about cars, but I'm pretty sure you don't want to touch that radiator cap." "Why?" he asked. I said it had to do with serious pain in your arm. He didn't believe me, so he grabbed a towel and put it over the radiator cap and loosened it just a little bit. Hot, hot steam started spewing out quickly. He retightened the cap and said, "Thanks for your advice. I think I will just let the engine cool down."

How many situations like that have you experienced over your lifetime? The older we get the more bits of wisdom we acquire. Part of our elderlescence stage of life is passing them on. But in reality there are many more significant contributions we have to offer to those who care to listen.

Let's think about practical places where you could share your wisdom with the younger generations. Try this exercise: write down a list of the top ten things that you are really good at and could share with others if you had the chance. Don't be too humble; this is the time to be honest and real. Solicit the help of your spouse or good life friend. Whatever you are good at, whatever you feel you can contribute to others, you have to find your delivery system. We will get more serious about venues in the later parts of the book, specifically chapter 19, but here are a few ideas now to whet your appetite:

- Teach classes at a local college.
- Teach classes at the community center.
- Teach classes in your local church.
- Start a new business venture.
- Volunteer with a mentoring program in your local church.
- Volunteer in the scouts.
- Volunteer in your area schools.
- Volunteer with mentoring programs in your community.
- Volunteer at your local community center.
- Get a part-time job.
- Help out in the local chapter of the Boys & Girls Club.
- Volunteer for a local nonprofit—they all need help.

Many boomers want to start a new encore career after their main careers are over. According to AARP, nine million Americans ages forty-four to seventy are engaged in second careers, and thirty-one million more are interested in pursuing one. In a survey conducted by encore.org and the MetLife Foundation, 25 percent of baby boomers hope to start a business or nonprofit in the next ten years. *They want to make a difference in the world while earning money*.[2] All this is ripe elderlescence experience.

In an article by Eric McWhinnie, this sentiment is clearly shared by the majority of boomers:

> Retirement is no longer viewed as a time to simply play shuffleboard or Bingo all day. Almost eighty percent of boomers expect to work in some capacity, even after they retire.

Fifty-one percent plan to work full-time, while twenty-eight say they expect to work part-time. However, many are using retirement as a chance to change careers.[3]

A lot of our wisdom comes from our life experience—like the radiator story. But as good as all this sounds, some of you reading this are skeptical. If there is one thing we have learned about aging people, it is that everyone is different. We know what some of you are thinking. *Yes, Hans and Rick, I do have a lot of wisdom, but I don't see anyone asking for it. They prefer to ask Google.* Google is great on facts but not so sharp on wisdom. We are going to explore in later chapters the venues you can find to share your wisdom with those who need to hear it from you. But, as in all the examples above, you will need to make the conscious choice to seek a platform for your influence. Unfortunately there are not a lot of people who know what you have to offer. So as uncomfortable as it might seem, you need to go out and sell yourself and find that place of contribution.

It's time to cash in your experience and find a platform for your new life. Marci Alboher, in her book *The Encore Career Handbook*, says that there is a collective feeling in our generation of "we're not done yet."[4] So if we're not done, let's get geared up for that next encore act.

You probably have more to share than you think—wisdom from your positive and negative life experiences that can benefit others. Can you help those who will come after you avoid falling into those same pits? We have all acquired a great deal of life wisdom from our years of experience. There are also other ways to acquire wisdom such as reading books, obtaining an education, and learning from others. A fast-track method of acquiring wisdom can be found in a source you may not have thought of. The book of Proverbs in the Bible is filled with the power of knowledge, understanding, and wisdom that resides within its pages. I, Rick, have been reading a chapter of Proverbs every day over the last several years. Since there are thirty-one chapters, it naturally correlates with the days of each month. So if today is the sixth of the month, I will begin my day by reading Proverbs 6. As a result of being exposed to these practical proverbs on such a repetitive basis over the years, I feel like I have absorbed God's wisdom into my heart of hearts. I am amazed at how often I can speak into people's lives and their issues with an exact quote from God's proverbs. I feel like I have the power of God's wisdom with me, which does way more than just dispensing my own understanding.

I challenge you to try reading a chapter of Proverbs every day. See what it offers in the very first chapter as it outlines a great promise:

> The proverbs of Solomon son of David, king of
>   Israel:
> for gaining wisdom and instruction;
>   for understanding words of insight;
> for receiving instruction in prudent behavior,
>   doing what is right and just and fair;
> for giving prudence to those who are simple,
>   knowledge and discretion to the young—
> let the wise listen and add to their learning,
>   and let the discerning get guidance—
> for understanding proverbs and parables,
>   the sayings and riddles of the wise.
> The fear of the LORD is the beginning of knowledge,
>   but fools despise wisdom and instruction. (vv. 1–7)

Elderlescence is a time of exploration. We hope you have a pioneer's spirit and are willing to do some good old-fashioned trial and error. You might not find your sweet spot the first time around, but don't give up. Keep looking for that place of contribution. Let's not put ourselves out to pasture just yet. Let's see the value of all we have learned and leverage it for good. Elderlescence is that later stage in your life when you utilize your experience and your knowledge to help bring along the next generations.

PART 2

The Choices
It Could Go Either Way

Wolfgang von Goethe said, "Whoever, in middle age, attempts to realize the wishes and hopes of his early youth invariably deceives himself. Each ten years of a life has its own fortunes, its own hopes, its own desires."[1] This new stage of life could blindside many of us. We often don't know what we don't know. The worst mistake is to be in neutral and assume life will keep working itself out.

There are two divergent paths we can choose: one of contribution or one of entitlement. If you are all about entitlement, you should probably toss this book at once!

For those of us who choose to pursue contribution in our later years of life, there is a wide range of possibilities. The key is to find *meaning* and *purpose* in this life stage. The goal in this pursuit is to discover positive ways to contribute back to society. The choice is yours.

If we choose to live an exclusively entitled lifestyle, we may lack fulfillment and may become a drain on society and our families. We might even end up in a very dark place. If we choose contribution, these years have the potential to be some of the most fulfilling times of our lives. Our final act might just be our greatest. This part of our book unpacks the intentionality of the journey, the urgency of creating this awareness, and clarity about the choices that we need to make. George Bernard Shaw said it so well:

> This is the true joy in life, the being used for a purpose recognized by yourself as a mighty one; the being a force of nature instead of a feverish selfish little clod of ailments and grievances complaining that the world will not devote itself to making you happy. I want to be thoroughly used up when I die, for the harder I work the more I live. I rejoice in life for its own sake. Life is no "brief candle" to me. It is a sort of splendid torch which I have got hold of for the moment, and I want to make it burn as brightly as possible before handing it on to future generations.[2]

Prepare for
6 the Choices Ahead

An old Cuban fisherman who lived by the sea was feeling that he had outlived his usefulness. Down on his luck, Santiago wasn't ready to give up his life on the sea. He knew he still had life left in him for another quest. And he felt he had few other options. But those around him were changing the way they treated him. This old man, who loved the sea, was increasingly being shunned by his community as a has-been. The younger fishermen were taking over. Santiago had so much passion left in him that he was prepared to go to the far ends of the Caribbean Gulf Stream to demonstrate that life was not over for him.

There are choices coming at us as we age that could be some of the greatest challenges we have ever faced. We need to recognize that we stand at this crossroads, and that the path we choose will set the capstone on our life. It could even define our legacy. If we passively follow the path of least resistance we may lose ground with each passing year. *We must intentionally find meaning and purpose—it might not find us.* That is the choice. Why is this quest for meaning and purpose so critical at this life stage? Why not just golf, enjoy our motorhome, and play with our grandkids?

If we back off on life and drift through our sixties and seventies we might come to a place of emptiness and despair, which we have described as the dark side. Maintaining high levels of meaning may become more difficult in old age due to the natural decline of health, income, physical well-being, and life losses. But there are many people, such as Jeanelle in chapter 4, who just don't throw in the towel on life.

Everyone who has researched aging agrees that *purpose in life* is always a key feature of good mental health. We haven't been talking about finding meaning and purpose just to fill space. It's actually the key to living a longer and healthier life. Christopher Borman and Patricia Henderson write in their article, "The Career/Longevity Connection," "Retirees at age 62 can expect to experience another 20–30 years of challenges and transactions in which purpose and meaning take on greater importance." The authors go on to say, "This is especially true because old age is a time when one's sources of meaning are at a greatest risk by virtue of the losses of personal relationships as well as the loss of career and community roles."[1]

As we focus on the choices around meaning and purpose, one of the great literary stories that comes to mind is that of *The Old Man and the Sea*, by Ernest Hemingway. There are many analogies to life in Hemingway's writings, but what jumps out at us in this book is his character Santiago's quest to find meaning and purpose in this concluding stage of his life. Santiago struggled with how he was viewed by those in his small fishing village. Did he still have worth, significance, and a sense of contribution to those in his life?

Santiago set out on his quest far into the Gulf Stream. After eighty-four days of fishing near his home without catching anything, he set out on his final quest farther than he had ever ventured before. In this story that is so rich in symbolism, the sea is a picture of life in general with all of its great rewards. Life is prepared to offer up great rewards to the diligent pursuer. Santiago kept in the hunt and caught the catch of a lifetime, a mighty marlin bigger than anything he had ever seen. But just like in life, the sharks came along to snatch away his victory. This great marlin he caught represents the treasure that awaits us in the sea of life, and the sharks symbolize the problems and defeats to be contended with.

What struck us was that a man of Santiago's age wasn't content to just live out his life without taking on another "life challenge." There was something driving him to continue to pursue his quest, to show he still had something to contribute to his village. It took incredible patience and courage to even start the task of going after the marlin. We don't know if Santiago was trying to prove he still had it in him or if he was just doing what he always did to have meaning and purpose in his life. What got him up in the morning, what he thought about all day long, was going out to sea. That is what fishermen do. After a long and tedious wait he finally hooked and landed the massive marlin, but the battle had just begun. There were additional challenges and threats, especially the sharks. Sounds a lot like normal life.

What we found revealing about this story is that no matter what our age we still have a longing to be significant, to engage, and to contribute. Many voices around us tell us that once we hit a certain age or station in life we should step back and let the younger generations take over. In some situations that may be true, but we should not allow others to sideline us before we are ready. Santiago proved to himself that he still had it in him, and in fact landed the biggest fish of his career in his aging years.

Let's not give in too quickly to those who want us sidelined because of the expectations of society. Whether we keep pursuing our "fishing" or choose new endeavors, we need to be responsible to make the choices that will keep bringing meaning and purpose to us.

Getting That Retirement Plan in Place

Santiago didn't have many choices other than fishing, but in today's world many of us do. He didn't really have a retirement plan, so he had to keep bringing in fish to pay his bills. We all have some critical choices we have to make to put us in a position to continue a fulfilling and meaningful life. Let's begin by focusing on our financial foundation for our future, because it is so foundational for everything else.

I, Rick, have been giving a lot of thought to what my wife, Kathy, and I need to do to have a purposeful 60–80 Window. We were advised to meet with a financial planner to help us think through the steps of getting our financial world in order for these next decades. When we sat down for this serious assessment, our eyes were opened to what we had been neglecting in preparation for our future. Our financial advisor is also a life transition specialist who helped us identify a number of areas that we needed to give attention to for our total well-being—not just money.

What we learned from this advisor was so helpful that we decided to include it in this chapter. We received permission from Mark Anderson and Joel Beyer to include a summary of their teaching on preparing for a successful financial future.[2] The full version can be downloaded on our website, www.launchyourencore.com. They base their principles on the teachings of the Bible, which we think is great advice for everyone. In fact we were blown away when we saw how much the Bible and Jesus talked about money.

Ten Biblical Principles for a Solid Financial Future

It's been said that the Bible contains over 2,300 verses that specifically deal with money and possessions. In fact, 15 percent of everything Jesus taught relates to this very subject. Regardless of your spiritual persuasion, you should recognize this advice as great words of wisdom.

1. Accept God's Ownership and Control

Everything in the heavens and earth is yours, O Lord, and this is your kingdom. We adore you as being in control of everything. (1 Chron. 29:11 TLB)

The Bible tells us that God owns and controls everything. Society tells us we are on our own, self-made, and self-important. Knowing that God is in complete control provides tremendous peace of mind in a world that often seems to be falling apart. He ultimately owns all our stuff; it's that plain and simple.

2. Learn True Contentment

I have learned to be content in whatever circumstances I am . . . in any and every circumstance I have learned the secret of being filled and going hungry, both of having abundance and suffering need. (Phil. 4:11–12 NASB)

The Bible tells us that godliness with contentment is great gain. Society tells us that we will only find satisfaction in obtaining more. The only problem is, more material wealth will never fill an empty heart. True contentment in our elder years is a great legacy to show our children and grandchildren.

3. Spend Less Than You Earn

The wise man saves for the future, but the foolish man spends whatever he gets. (Prov. 21:20 TLB)

This one should be a no-brainer. Chronic overspending is a real problem in our society. It is often a sign of spiritual discontentment and can ultimately lead to ever-increasing debt—even divorce or bankruptcy. The "more is better" way of life is full of stress, conflict, and disappointment. Credit cards and consumer borrowing give all of us a license to consume regardless of the balance in our checkbook, an unwise course for everyone.

4. Minimize the Use of Debt

Just as the rich rule the poor, so the borrower is servant to the lender. (Prov. 22:7 TLB)

There is no question that debt can be crippling. Debt is often the byproduct of overspending, which is often a byproduct of lack of contentment. Left unchecked, debt can bring down countries (Argentina), cities (Detroit), corporations (Lehman Brothers), and families. Debt is not sin in and of itself, but debt can be a fearful master. For some, borrowing is just an easy way out of a situation that would otherwise force us to grow in our faith and character.

5. Plan for the Future

The plans of the diligent lead surely to plenty,
But those of everyone who is hasty, surely to poverty.
(Prov. 21:5 NKJV)

Many people have told us that they avoid planning because "things never work out the way I planned." This may be true. But the reason to plan is not because a plan will always unfold perfectly; it's to get our minds and actions aligned with our ultimate objectives.

> "Would you tell me, please, which way I ought to go from here?" asked Alice.
> "That depends a good deal on where you want to get to," said the Cat.
> "I don't much care where—" said Alice.
> "Then it doesn't matter which way you go," said the Cat.[3]

Planning is the act of reviewing and organizing all elements and potential actions involved in achieving a goal or objective. Careful planning can save many hours of implementation. The first step is to clarify and define values and goals. Setting meaningful goals is the start of a great financial plan.

6. Seek Wise Counsel

> The way of a fool is right in his own eyes,
> But a wise man is he who listens to counsel.
> (Prov. 12:15 NASB)

No person is an island of all knowledge. We can fall into a trap where we believe that just because we may have expert skills and experience in a certain profession or vocation we are automatically a qualified expert in another. Nothing could be further from the truth.

Most people avoid counsel for three reasons:

Pride: We think we are so smart that we can figure everything out by reading a book or a magazine or through an internet search. Pride hides significant blind spots in our judgment, and can lead us into making many foolish mistakes.

Fear: We feel we should know more about a particular subject, and are embarrassed to have the world discover how little we really know. So we sometimes refuse to do anything, despite the potential risks.

Selfishness: All too often we want our own way, and we don't want to be talked out of it. The wisest people we know seek counsel from trusted experts. They are intelligent and open to ideas that may not always fit their feelings—because they know they are not experts in every subject. Imagine how much heartache, stress, and trouble you could have avoided over the years, if only you would have sought and heeded wise and experienced counsel.

7. Invest Long-Term, Diversify, and Do Not Speculate

Steady plodding brings prosperity; hasty speculation brings poverty. (Prov. 21:5 TLB)

When we are younger, investing can help us build future security and freedom. When we are in our "capstone" years, investing may be more about providing an inflation-adjusted income that we can live from for the rest of our days. Nobody knows with certainty what "investment" will outperform in the future. Nobody. The Bible tells us that patience and discipline are the keys to successful investing. It's the tortoise principle, not the hare. (Please review the full document at www .launchyourencore.com for a full discussion of this point.)

8. Give Generously

> Honor the LORD with your possessions,
> And with the firstfruits of all your increase.
> (Prov. 3:9 NKJV)

The Bible tells us to give generously of God's resources. Society teaches us that charity begins at home and that he who dies with the most toys wins. In his book *Managing God's Money*, Randy Alcorn reminds us that giving is a form of grace. We love because God first loved us, and we give because he first gave to us. Since everything belongs to him and there is no limit to his desire to entrust more into the hands of his most generous givers, why would we want to be anything other than lavishly generous with his resources?

9. Pass On a Living Legacy

> A good man leaves an inheritance to his children's children. (Prov. 13:22 NKJV)

Certainly in Old Testament times, when wealth consisted of land and animals, the only way the next generation could survive was to inherit family property. Even so, God warned against too much wealth being passed too easily. "An inheritance gained hastily at the beginning will not be blessed at the end" (Prov. 20:21 NKJV). The results of such unrestrained wealth transfers often include untold amounts of wasted wealth, as well as the devastation of wasted lives given over to addictive and immoral lifestyles.

Henry Ford observed that "fortunes tend to self-destruction by destroying those who inherit them."[4] While society in general teaches us to leave as much wealth to our heirs as we can to make their lives easier, the Bible teaches the only legacy worth leaving is a legacy that passes biblical principles for living God-honoring lives. To pass wealth without the biblical tools for wise management is like giving a teenager the keys to the car without first teaching him or her how to drive.

10. Set Your Estate in Order

Set your house in order, for you shall die. (2 Kings 20:1 NKJV)

God's warning to King Hezekiah through the prophet Isaiah is the same kind of warning he gives all of us. Death is coming, so we would all be well advised to set our estates in order. And since none of us knows the day and time of our passing, the prudent thing to do would be to get it done sooner rather than later. Failure to do so is to ignore what could be the most profound single act of stewardship most of us will ever make.

Two Stories

We asked our two friends who wrote up these ten principles to give us a story of success and a story of failure. There are those who listen to good advice and make plans for the future, and those who, sadly, do not. There are plenty of both scenarios. We'll start with the bad news and end on a positive note.

Failure Story from Mark

While most of us wholeheartedly believe in the wisdom of writing a will or a trust, most Americans die without so much as a note of instruction scribbled on a napkin (and I have seen a few of those in my day).

Several years ago a man in his eighties came into my office and begged me to help him provide for his only son, who was caught up in a lifestyle of drug and alcohol abuse. When I outlined a plan to safeguard his wealth using a trust language designed to encourage his son to make better life decisions (allowing access to money for rehabilitation and educational pursuits), the man thanked me and promised to call back in a few weeks to get started. But he never did. Unfortunately, the man died a few weeks ago and now his son (still obviously struggling with his addictions) is going to receive access to wealth that he is not only wholly ill-equipped to manage but which will very likely hasten his death.

Success Story from Joel

Perhaps the most inspiring success story of following biblical financial success principles was with a young couple I'll call the Johnsons. I have worked with the Johnsons for over ten years. Over this time, I have seen Mr. Johnson work his way up the corporate ladder in a large, well-known technology company. His hard work and faithfulness have propelled him into a leadership role in his company and his selfless sacrifice has positioned him as a hero to his family. There is so much more about this family that I could tell you, about both Mr. and Mrs. Johnson and their children. God has rewarded this family's faithfulness exceedingly over time.

What has impressed me the most about the Johnsons is their intelligence combined with their willingness to follow expert advice. Over the years they have followed all of the biblical principles we have outlined. They spend less than they earn, and as a result they have avoided the use of debt, are able to give generously, and have invested a substantial portion of their income for the future. They have a solid plan in place, are well prepared for retirement, and have everything in perfect order for the time and place when God takes them from this world. I couldn't have made up a more perfect "by the book" success story.

Finally

No one wants to leave a legacy filled with would have, could have, should have. We don't know anyone who wants to be remembered for all of his or her bad decisions. This final stretch can and should be a time for smooth sailing and finishing strong. We hope you will take these ten principles seriously. And we really hope you will seek wise counsel and find true contentment in the process.

7 Great Expectations

Bill and Diane decided to sell their home in Colorado and move to North Carolina to be close to their grandkids. Being involved in the lives of their grandchildren was the deciding factor for the move. They sold their beautiful ranch and bought a spacious home in the same neighborhood as their children. In their plans, they wanted to be sure that there was plenty of room in the house for the grandkids to roam. But not many months went by before the sparks began to fly between Grandpa and Grandma and Mom and Dad. The grandparents desired meals together as a family more often than was comfortable for their children and grandchildren. Bill and Diane also wanted to be involved in many aspects of their grandchildren's community life and sports activities, and they had plenty of financial resources to lavish on these grandkids.

With all of these expectations from the grandparents, it came to a point where serious conflict took place. Their children got to the point where they wished their parents had not moved into such close proximity. Finally, through a very painful encounter, the children confronted their parents and insisted on establishing realistic boundaries for Grandpa and Grandma. The confrontation was devastating to Bill and Diane. These boundaries felt like a slap in the face. "How can our kids put these kinds of rules on us, their parents? We came here to help and love our grandkids and be in their lives."

This story is just one illustration of how unmet expectations can derail our plans at this stage of our life. Nothing creates more conflict and disappointment in life than unmet expectations. Many of us who become grandparents have felt some of the unmet expectations of involvement with our children and grandchildren. We have to navigate not only the expectations of our children but also the other set of grandparents, who have their own set of desires. Things don't always get as extreme as the story of Bill and Diane, but a lot of us can relate to these kinds of hurts and disappointments.

By the way, after the confrontation the families worked it out and Grandpa and Grandma agreed with the boundaries. They actually found other meaningful things to do in North Carolina in their retirement years.

If you unpack any conflict, up to and including warfare between countries, you can boil it down to disagreement about expectations of what the other party should be doing or how they should behave. When we are creating our encore in later life, conflict can even erupt within our own psyche, as we think *I am not where I thought I would be at this place in my life. I am not where I want to be. I'm not sure what is next. What do I do now?*

Our life at this stage can be filled with great satisfaction because we are who we thought we would become. But for many others, there can be a growing, bitter disappointment that we did not fulfill our own personal expectations of ourselves. "I did not become what I had hoped." "I stayed in that rut of a job too long." "I never got that promotion I worked so hard for." "I can't believe they just dumped me after all those years I gave them." And for many of us, "I did not set aside enough for my retirement years."

When we face later-life transitions, it is time to take an honest look at what realistic expectations we should entertain as we enter the 60–80 Window. What can we dream to become, or what is a setup for failure? In our experience, it is a redefining time when expectations have to be tweaked and retweaked. How do we do that? We find that some people are really good at projecting their potential going forward, but many of us have blind spots that need help. Peer feedback from family and trusted friends will be an essential piece of creating a plan that has a good chance of success.

I, Hans, want to illustrate how I handled this in my major post-career life transition. When I reached age sixty, after twenty years as a nonprofit CEO, I sensed it was time to move on. I didn't know where I needed to go next, but I was sure I needed to change things up. I had lost my passion for my job, and a CEO needs to be all in or all gone. It was a frightening experience and a transition that lasted several years, but I knew I had to step out and create a new future. It was not a move into retirement, though I did retire from a career and organization I had been with for thirty-two years. To me it was a retirement from a main-act career into a new second career, working for myself.

Isn't it amazing how different we are when we are sixty as opposed to fifty or forty? We have different desires, motivations, interests, and even capabilities. Everyone's different. I have friends who are still maximizing their output and performance in the same position well into their seventies. But for me, it was time for a change. So now the question became, "What will I do next?" One thing is for sure, when we are forty there are a lot of options and we are very marketable. A lot of people will help us find our dream jobs. When we are in our sixties and beyond, not so much. *It is a time when we have to work hard ourselves at creating our encore.*

Donna and I were advised by some trusted friends to form a group that could help us in this major later-in-life career transition. We sought a small, trusted peer feedback community that could help us make the right decisions about our next step. We ended up calling this group the TAG team: *transition, affirmation,* and *guidance.* It was a group of four people, all of whom we have known for decades. They know us, they love us, and they believe in us. Speaker and consultant William Bridges says we should ask these questions: "What do I really want at this point in my life? Not what I used to want but what I want now. Not silly wishes like living on a boat in Mexico. But things I could do realistically." And he explains that we are highly motivated by "wants." "What do I really *want* at this time in my life?"[1]

I'll never forget one day when I was putting on a baseball cap made by the folks at Life Is Good. Sewn inside the cap are these words, which come into view when you place the cap on your head: "Do what you like, like what you do." I read those words and said to myself, *I am doing neither.* It was time for a change. That baseball cap changed my life. That is the cool thing about the encore of our lives—we can work it out so we can do what we love and love what we do. Some people we know have been waiting for decades for just this moment.

Once I decided I needed a change, Donna and I organized our TAG team and went to work. Over a period of a year and a half, as I was transitioning out of my former job, we met together periodically to review options, evaluate opportunities, and map out a healthy and realistic new career that would match my passions with my activities. I knew I could not afford to retire, but at this stage in my life I wanted to find a job that I loved.

Our TAG team began by making me drill down deep into my heart and list those things that fuel me and give me the greatest satisfaction. The list included things I feel that I am gifted in and good at. For some people it can be continuing the same career in a different manner, but for others it can be an exciting ninety-degree turn into something outlandishly new, like the engineer who retired and opened that Italian pizza joint he had always wanted to pursue. Then there are people who just love spending more time with their grandkids, like my friend who told me the other day, "When I retire, Hans, I want to take my grandchildren to school every morning and pick them up afterward." I'm not convinced that's going to be enough for my friend, but it certainly speaks to the passion of his heart.

The more we believe in what we're doing, the easier it is to have passion. The less we love what we do, the more it shows on the outside. Webster defines *passion* as deriving from the Latin word *pati*, "to suffer." That is where the idea of the passion of Christ comes from. Passion is "a strong feeling of enthusiasm or excitement for something or about doing something. Intense, driving, or overmastering feeling or conviction."[2]

That explains why passion is so critical as we create our expectations of the future and our encore. Confucius was the first to observe, "Choose a job you love, and you will never have to work another day in your life."[3] My friend Tom has a great way to gauge how close you are to working in your passion. He asks, "If you won the lottery tomorrow, what would you do with the rest of your life?" If you've been fortunate enough to create a financial safety net, where creating more income is not necessary, then it does come down to the question of what you would do that you love at this stage in your life.

To round out the issue of expectations, we have to state the obvious: Our society has expectations of a somewhat formal retirement at age sixty-six, tied to our Social Security retirement age. So new choices end up getting imposed on many of us by default. Even if we try to hang on to our past life, many of us are squeezed out, pushed out, shoved out, or iced out. We get forced into the retirement zone whether we like it or not. When that happens, the first task is to get over it. Even Jay Leno had to walk that journey.

In an article titled "Success and Achievement in Old Age— Why You are Never Too Old to Succeed," there is a great observation about the prejudice against old age in our society.

> There are a lot of assumptions and prejudice according to age. It is assumed that aging occurs in a somewhat linear fashion, and is something guaranteed. However, a careful look around society will show the clear variety of people with different ages, abilities, and stamina. Not all people are the same, and no two people age the same either. . . . The main problem faced by older people, however, is the stereotypes that they face . . . it is unfortunate that many individuals might be pushed toward a retirement that they are not entirely ready for. In fact, the perception that over a certain age a person is "past it" is a hindrance in itself.[4]

Questions Surrounding Your Great Expectations

We want to finish this chapter by giving you a challenge to work on your own expectations. We all have choices to make based on healthy, realistic expectations of who we are at this stage of our lives. If you won the lottery, what would you do with your time? When you reach the later-life stage of post-career, how would you configure an ideal future? Of course, your choices can be full-time, part-time, or intermittent. Here are some questions you should consider asking yourself. They all circle around the idea of passion. As we live through the 60–80 Window, this should absolutely be the time when we "do what we love and love what we do." You will also find these four questions in chapter 20, where we lay out the complete guide to launching your encore.

1. *Current situation: What are you doing right now to fill your time?* Make a list of all the things that seem to be filling your calendar. Then next to each item put a number by the level of passion/satisfaction that you get out of that activity, on a scale of 1 to 10. One means no passion, and ten means there's nothing you'd rather be doing. For example, "I take care of my grandkids every Wednesday." I have a dear friend who does that every week, and he just smiles and comes alive when he tells me about it. The first step in any assessment is to take a look at what you are doing now.

2. *What fuels you?* As you look back over your life, make a list of the things that you most enjoyed doing. They could be activities, hobbies, aspects of your profession, or anything else. What are you passionate about? What lights you up? When you do these things you sense God's pleasure. Like Eric Liddell, the famous Olympic athlete, who said, "I believe God made me for a purpose, but he also made me fast. And when I run I feel his pleasure."[5]

3. *What are your dreams about your future?* Now let's dream about the future. Will it include your dream job? Whether they pay you or not, you'd love to do this.

Make a list of all the things you love to fill your calendar with. Go crazy. Fill your list with fun, passion, and satisfaction.

4. *Reality check: What do others think?* Now let's talk about realistic expectations. Ask for input. Just as our TAG team helped Donna and me solidify our passion and direction, go there! Just ask. In the meantime, consider this: If you were to ask your spouse or trusted friends what they think you should do, what are things you think or know they would mention?

We encourage you to consider your expectations about your future carefully. Doing this exercise related to these four questions can go a long way in helping you prepare for what lies ahead. The more you can align your expectations in a positive way that matches who you are and your circumstances, the more fulfilling an experience you can have in your encore years. We desire to see you set yourself up for great success.

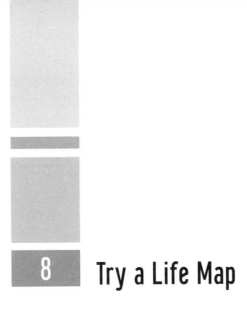

8 Try a Life Map

Rick, have been part of teaching a mentoring clinic for the last eight years. As we help people reach their God-given potential, one of the most significant tools we use is the life map. For me, personally, going through this exercise was incredibly revealing for the shape, pattern, and direction of my life. As I drew out my life on a big piece of butcher paper, I was able to see the high and low points of my life. This tool helped me identify times of success and failure, and helped me make more sense of my life story. One of my colleagues who teaches this section of our clinic is Elke Hanssmann, a real expert in mentoring and life transitions. We have asked her to write this chapter on life mapping and what it means to her personally.

Life Mapping by Elke Hanssmann

I woke up at 3:15 a.m., bathed in cold sweat, and could feel my heart pounding. Thoughts were racing through my mind.

The recurring sentences, like a broken record, were *I just can't do this. I just can't do this! When it's morning I am going to call my new boss and tell him I won't be coming.* I was about to start a completely new chapter in my life, which required me to move to a new country and start a new job that had not existed before, but which had been carefully designed and tailored to utilize my gifts and skills to the maximum. But I was scared and paralyzed with fear to start over again. Then in the midst of my fear of the future there was another voice, the gentle whisper from God, *Do you remember. . . . You felt like this before. You've been here before . . . and not only did you make it through, you actually loved it!*

Thus is the power of remembering. Numerous times in the Bible (for example, Deut. 8:2; Josh. 4:6–7; Ps. 77), we find an exhortation to stop and look back over our lives, to stop and remember.

Why is that so important? Reviewing our story can build our faith and instill courage to step into the future. As you consider composing your future life, in many ways you are starting with a blank canvas where nothing has been pre-painted or outlined. At the same time, you do not start from nothing but bring with you a tremendous treasure chest of past experience. We all do, but not everybody sits down to take out the jewels and pearls that are hidden within that chest.

There is a powerful tool that can serve to unlock the future for you like few other things might—a personal lifeline/life map. This is a way to think about your life from a helicopter perspective, gaining an overview over the whole of your life as you have lived it up to now. Leonie Sugarman observes, "Despite the changes that beset all of us as we grow up and grow older, we do not become totally different people."[1] There are changes, for sure, but also a real sense of continuity. Taking an all-life approach to reviewing your life might evidence surprising patterns and bring out values, principles, gifts, character traits, and skills that run through your life like a thread. These threads might provide useful information for you and the crossroads you find yourself at. Often past behavior, choices, preferences, and experiences can be reliable guides for the future.

With our team at OM, I have facilitated countless mentoring and coaching workshops for more than eight years in nations all across the globe. As part of equipping those mentors, we aid them in developing their own life maps. And without fail, both writing and sharing their personal life journey maps rank among the highlights of the workshop.

What are the benefits of actually taking some time to write down our experiences and reflect a bit more deeply on them? What makes this such a powerful tool? Graham Lee suggests that "Links between personal history and present circumstances are often profound and potentially transformative."[2] Reviewing your life can not only give you new insights on your current circumstances but also transform your perspective, giving you new perspective on the choices you have taken and the importance of key decisions, milestones, and achievements in your life. This process also enables you to take a new perspective on perceived mistakes and failures, thus freeing you to leave unnecessary baggage behind as you walk into the future. And who of us would not like to travel lighter?

An examination of personal history can help us identify patterns that have served us well and might be worth taking into the new future with us. They might also help us shed those patterns that rendered us ineffective! The Bible invites us to "make a careful exploration of who you are and the work you have been given," and not to compare ourselves with others (ever so tempting for most of us!) but to "take responsibility for doing the creative best you can with your own life" (Gal. 6:4–5 Message).

A life map is exactly that—a way to carefully explore creation design: What did God put into the gift box of my life—what gifts, temperament, talents, values, and so forth keep coming through as I review my life? How has God made me, and how can I do the creative best with it in my new life stage? It builds confidence of "this is me," releasing us from the temptation to compare ourselves with others whose choices might be very different based on who they are and what life has taught them.

So, in reviewing your story, what are some benefits you can expect from a life map?

- It gives an overall pattern of God's work in your life—and leads to praise and thankfulness. As a result of that, it gives faith and courage to step into the future.
- It gives a much larger perspective than just the "now" slice of your life—which is key for making future long-term decisions.
- It helps identify values and convictions (which will serve as a filter for future choices—criteria for the decision-making process).
- It instills hope for the future as you remember how you overcame fears, barriers, and obstacles in the past.
- It enables you to avoid repeating mistakes you have made in the past.
- It helps bring out recurring strengths and weaknesses.
- It clarifies vision, dreams, and areas of calling in your life.

Many of my coaching clients seek me out at transitional points in their lives. Unsure as to where to go from here, they often only know that they find themselves at a crossroads in life and are looking for a safe travel companion to help them make wise choices. Often their life map brings out key insights that take away the fog and give clarity for their next steps.

Hopefully this has convinced you that the time necessary to create your own life map is well invested. So—let's get started. Here is an overview of the steps of a life map:

1. Brainstorming your history.
2. Creating your map—putting it all together.
3. Making sense of it all.
4. Dividing into past, present, and future chapters.

Your Personal Life Map

1. Brainstorming Your History

This is to include all of your life, and there are various ways you can go about this. You can choose to create a thematic map (career choices, major life decisions, achievements, milestones) or just include all themes together to make a more comprehensive and richer multifaceted map. I would recommend including as much as you can to get as much depth and breadth as possible. Some categories to brainstorm about:

a. *People.* Who were significant people who left their mark in your life? Positive role models, mentors, people who inspired you or helped you at significant points in your life. Also include negative people—people who influenced you for the worse, damaged you, whom you'd rather forget but who clearly influenced you, if only that you decided you never wanted to be like them. Authority figures, parents, family members, bosses, and colleagues—what messages did they speak into your life, how did they shape you, what did you integrate from them into your life?

b. *Significant events.* What would be marker events that somehow shaped your life? It could be things like your graduation day, the day you moved houses as a child, the death of a loved one, your first date with the person who is now your spouse. Start listing events that in your mind have been significant in your life journey, and then reflect a bit more about why these would stand out in your mind. How did they affect you? Maybe you learned the importance of initiating after making a move and starting over—skills and abilities that now might come in handy. Perhaps you have skills you were not even aware you had, which have been developing throughout your life.

c. *Key decisions you made.* As you look back over your life, list some important decisions you have made that were of consequence. It could be as big as choosing a career path or as small as deciding to no longer wait to be discovered but to start being more proactive. After listing the decisions themselves, start identifying the drivers behind those decisions. This is starting to help you connect with key values you hold and patterns of decisions that set your life in motion. The likelihood of these values and drivers displaying continuity through-out the changes of your life is high, and can serve as another filter to help you weigh options for composing the future.

d. *Turning points.* Try to recall those times in your life when things really changed, when core assumptions were challenged, when you made significant shifts, or something was very different afterward. Often these turning points align with personal transitions or bigger crises in life. I recall a deeper crisis of faith during my nursing training, where the fragility of life shook me to the core and drove me to look for things that were of lasting meaning and value. From that point onward, I chose to invest in things that would last, a choice that runs like a thread throughout the rest of my career choices.

e. *Moments of feeling fully alive.* These will be a bit harder to recall, but it's worth the effort. When and where in your life did you feel you were at your best, using all your capacities and feeling what Mihaly Csikszentmihalyi describes as *flow*—being fully immersed in something, fully energized, and enjoying the process, and time just flies.[3] Many of us call this living in our "sweet spot." As you recall those moments, take the time to analyze them and break them down into components. What made them energizing? What were you doing? What skills were you using? What kind of environment did you find yourself in? Who else was there? What was actually happening? Dissecting these experiences can greatly help you in answering the question, "What would my ideal context look like in which I would naturally flourish?"

f. *Disappointments, failures, mistakes made.* While these might be less pleasant to remember, they still offer a rich source of insight. We tend to learn far more from our mistakes than our successes. So as you call to mind the times you'd rather forget, elicit what these times have done in shaping you. One of my most painful years ever was when I was coleading a church-planting team in my midtwenties, in post-communist Germany. The toxic mix of being clueless about church planting itself and team leadership, while being too insecure and proud to ask for help, led to me writing this year off as a massive failure never to be repeated. It was only years later, when I did one of my first life maps, that I started seeing how this particular experience, painful as it had been, had ignited a passion within me to see leaders well equipped, trained, and supported for the responsibilities they were entrusted with. Flowing out of my failure have come years of developing emerging high-potential leaders, global leaders, and women in leadership roles, all fueled by my own painful experience. We easily discard what seems shameful and painful—yet as Richard Rohr insightfully observes, "The place of the wound is the place of healing. The place of the break is the place of the greatest strength."[4] Often the fault line turns out to be the strongest point!

g. *Jobs, careers, education.* This will give you a much more straightforward list of skills and qualifications. As you consider the different jobs you held and career paths you pursued throughout your life, draw out the commonalities. What was required in all of them? Which ones did you most enjoy or find yourself most successful in?

h. *Successes and accomplishments.* What are the things you achieved in life that you are really proud of? And what does this say about you? What principles can you draw from those that are applicable to your future direction? These can be in sports, academics, the arts, professionally, or any other field. Brainstorm all you can think of. Maybe it was running a marathon and the attitudes of perseverance and discipline that you can now apply to creating your next chapter in life. Maybe it was learning a language or making a life in a new country and the need to initiate and be innovative that can be transferred to your next challenge. For me, moving to Spain and learning to survive and build a life in a foreign country without knowing a word of Spanish required perseverance and initiative. Six years later I was fluent, with a circle of friends, and cried my eyes out when I moved away from there. The skill of persevering in overcoming obstacles was something I transferred into numerous new challenges, as several times in my life I had to reinvent my context and career.

There are numerous other categories that could be considered. What follows is a brief, nonexclusive list of pointers, all of which can add more layers and dimensions to your detective work:

Significant places (geography)
Hobbies and interests
Gifts, talents, and skills
Books that shaped you
Obstacles overcome
Family influences
Highlights and low points
Regrets
Main temptations and traps
Unique opportunities

2. Creating Your Map—Putting It All Together

Now that you have collected the puzzle pieces of your life, you can start putting things together in a cohesive fashion. Actually creating your life map can be as simple as taking a large sheet of butcher paper and drawing a line across the middle of it, symbolizing your birth at one end of the paper and your current point in life at the other end. Above the line you can add what you perceive as positive experiences, below the more challenging ones. This will appeal to more linear people. If you are less linear, something like a mind map, a cluster diagram, a collage, or an image like "the garden of my life" might appeal more. There are no limits to your creativity, as long as it serves the purpose of helping you elicit the different strands of the tapestry of your life so that you can weave the next chapter into it! I have seen some amazing samples in my workshops, from "monopoly of life" to a "snakes and ladders" board game chart over a topographical life map, colorful collages, and trees with roots and shoots. Let your creativity flow. You can also Google "creative life map ideas" for inspiration. Here is one example of a linear life map.

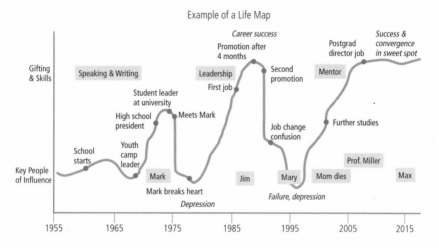

Example of a Life Map

3. Making Sense of It All

Now that you have created your map, let it serve you. What does it tell you about your life up to now? What could be useful ingredients for composing a future life? What patterns do you see emerging? Repetitive themes? If you are a Christian, what are ways that God has been leading you so far? And what are your principles of guidance? What has helped you navigate other crossroads in your life, and how can you apply that to your current choices? What does your life map tell you about your future and the "ideal" life for you, using what you have to offer to its maximum, and building on previous experience? Taking the time to share your map with a trusted friend who is a good listener might also reveal additional insights and give you pointers that aid decision-making processes. This might also be a good place to consult a professional life direction/transition coach. A neutral pair of eyes might spot what familiar eyes might easily overlook. Here is a slice of the life map that Hans made recently.

Years	Age	Key Events/People	Insights
1974	23	Moved to Columbia Graduated from CIU Called into ministry Began at Dallas Theological Seminary Parental disappointment: mother did not come to graduation	Life imprint: master, mate, and mission Became a leader on campus and my leadership gifts were shown
1975	24	Courtship and wedding to Donna	Started a new life without my independence Adjustment to married life Off to a great start in the little apartment at the Purnells
1974–78	23–26	Dallas Seminary (DTS) Newlyweds	Moved to DTS and had a great journey there in training and preparation for ministry Excelled in school Had fun as newly married
1978	27	Graduated from DTS Moved to California Donna at Oilwell	Launch of our career Enjoyed the years before kids Had a lot of fun in California

4. Dividing into Past, Present, and Future Chapters

After carefully exploring your life map, another way to gain further insight is by dividing the map into "life chapters." For example, Hudson and McLean have created an exercise where you divide your life into chapters, clearly indicating the starting and ending dates of each chapter—and why each chapter ends where it does.[5]

This exercise will help you tie your experiences up to now into segments that might correlate with some of your life stages. Our hopes, desires, and priorities tend to change as our lives progress, and future chapters might provide continuity with the past while at the same time also introducing new priorities and fulfilling new desires. Carl Gustav puts it well in *Modern Man in Search of a Soul*:

> Thoroughly unprepared, we take the step into the afternoon of life. Worse still, we take this step with the false presupposition that our truths and our ideals will serve us as hitherto. But we cannot live the afternoon of life according to the program of life's morning, for what was great in the morning will be little at evening and what in the morning was true, at evening will have become a lie.[6]

So—after dividing your map into chapters, why not take a clean sheet of paper and start authoring in your mind what the next chapter may look like? Who would you like to be the main characters in that chapter? What storyline would you like? What values would you like to live out that maybe have run through your life like a theme song, or equally might have been suppressed by necessities of life that no longer constrain you? How can your strengths and previous experience really begin to shine in the coming chapter? Allow yourself to dream as a vision of your encore starts to emerge. This map is not complete; keep it handy, for we will pull it out again in chapter 20 when we're putting it all together!

If you go to our website, www.launchyourencore.com, you will find some more illustrations of variations on the theme of how to draw a life map. Be creative and do it your own way. If you have just read this chapter without completing any of the exercises, let us assure you that there are no shortcuts to composing your future life. Taking the time to work through your life in the fashion Elke described will empower you to walk into your future with a much stronger sense of hope, direction, and choice!

Old Dogs Can Learn
9 New Tricks

Over at the Finzel household, we've always loved Discovery Channel's hit show *MythBusters*, in which a team of experts put common adages and folklore to the test of science (and have a lot of fun doing it). In the episode "Dog Myths," the team successfully taught two old and notoriously difficult-to-train dogs a series of new tricks, definitively busting the myth once and for all: you really can teach an old dog new tricks. And we are so glad that they proved that one for us.

Thomas Jefferson observed, "Though an old man I am but a young gardener."[1] After all his public glory, he learned new tricks in his later, quiet years out of the public eye, including gardening. At this encore stage of our life, we more than likely have to learn new life skills. If we want to make the best of our encore, we need to learn some new tricks. Sometimes the new skills we learn are very close to things we did in our career, but even then there are some new developmental tasks we all have to deal with.

The other day I, Hans, was shopping at Trader Joe's in Chicago while traveling. The gentleman helping me check out was obviously in his mid- to late seventies. He exuded confidence and dignity. I struck up a conversation with him. I asked him, "What did you do in your former life?" I don't usually go around asking people that, but he seemed very friendly and I wondered about his life story. I could just tell there was an interesting story here. He said, "I was an engineer and a consultant for my whole career. After I retired I became bored; now I work here for golf money. I couldn't stand just being around the house all the time, and I love working here. And my wife is happy to have me gone for some of the time each week. The company encourages us to relate to customers and to not just hurry people through the checkout line. I never thought I would love coming to work at a grocery store!" Here was a dignified old dog who had learned some great new tricks.

Every life stage has developmental tasks that have to be mastered. As teenagers, we had to learn what it meant to navigate adolescence and learn new tasks, such as how to drive. Now, at this stage, we have to become familiar and at home in elderlescence. It can be done, but it does take intentionality. We don't need to fear what lies ahead as long as we realistically approach life aware of our new limitations. The best defense is a great offense.

We have noticed that in our sixties we are having new life issues thrown at us that we have to cope with. Many of us are dealing with elderly, ailing parents. We're also seeing our children leave the nest and start their own families. We become in-laws to our kids' spouses and grandparents. Physical issues begin to show up, related to our health and vitality. Then some of us struggle with cognitive issues as we find our minds are not as sharp as they were when we were younger. I have a good friend, Scott, in his early sixties, who bumped his head and endured a brain injury that set him back for two years. "I felt like a kid starting over in life, and my mouth could not keep up with my brain as I tried to talk," he told me. Scott struggled a lot with his own self-worth as he struggled to learn how to talk again. At this stage of life such limitations have a double impact because people start treating us like the fragile elderly—not how we want to be treated!

We find that we have dear life friends and family members struggling with terrible diseases. We lose peers and family members to death. Of course financial realities change dramatically for many of us. Are you getting the picture of the train coming down the tracks toward us whether we like it or not? There is no stopping these realities; the issue is coping, adjusting, and learning new life skills.

We all want to grow old happy. Happiness is important to maintain in our later years, and can be greatly affected by expectations. After reviewing the results of a major research project by the Pew Research Center, scientists strongly suspect that expectations and the ability to adapt to changing life circumstances greatly influence happiness. "People who adjust their expectations as their social networks and lifestyles change may avoid feelings of loneliness and isolation, which are linked to illness and earlier death."[2]

New Life Skills to Explore

Let's explore a list of life stage tasks we have come up with for ages sixty to eighty, and answer a few questions such as: How do I fit into life now? What new skills do I need for this stage of my life? What decisions are out there staring at us?

Where Will We Live?

This is a question we all face. Do we move into a smaller home? Donna and I were discussing this with our family not long ago, and they were all against it. Our children love our home where they grew up, and have a great sentimental attachment to it. But we have to think about accessibility and mobility as we grow older. Do we get a house that will be more manageable when we are more physically restrained? And do we stay in the same city where we have been, or do we move closer to our children and grandchildren? Most people say you shouldn't chase your children around the country to live near them, because they keep moving. However, that's not always the best advice. It's a good idea in the later years of your life to be near family who can be there for you. This is a big decision that all of us face sooner or later.

Where we will choose to locate later in life revolves around many issues. The big three that we see driving us to move are being near our children and grandchildren, finding a better climate, and living in an area with a lower cost of living.

How Do We Adjust Our Lifestyle Based on Our Financial Realities?

Of course we have to talk about money. We bring it up again since it is such a critical life stage task for us. When we reach those retirement income years, what sort of a budget will we be able to live on? What will our income and our expenses be? How will that affect our lifestyle? I know you're probably getting tired of all these questions, but they are real. The train is on the tracks, heading straight for us. Again, we believe that a good offense is the best defense.

According to the Employee Benefit Research Institute, 13 percent of workers who delayed retirement in 2011 said they did so because of "inadequate finances or can't afford to retire" and 6 percent did so because of "needing to make up for losses in the stock market."[3] The results of the 2013 Retirement Confidence Survey, the nation's longest-running annual retirement survey, put on by the Employee Benefit Research Institute, illustrated different numbers but similar trends in attitudes when its results were released in March 2013. This survey is a random, nationally representative survey of one thousand individuals age twenty-five and over, and it too reported "a sharp decline in Americans' confidence about their ability to secure a financially comfortable retirement."[4]

What Is Our Relationship with Our Family Now?

The empty nest provides the opportunity to change our relationship with our children. How do we relate to them now? What do they want and need from us? There are those horror stories like Bill and Diane's, but there are more great stories of success in this arena. Donna and I are blessed to have four children. They are choosing wonderful spouses and their marriages are giving us a growing group of grandchildren (five and counting). But we often discuss the question, "How can we be involved in the lives of our children and grandchildren without invading their privacy as they raise their own families?" We want to be in their lives, but our role is different. Navigating our relationships with our children, our grandchildren, and our aging parents is very much a part of the new skills of this life stage. It wouldn't hurt to discuss these expectations with our family members, just as Bill and Diane finally had to do after damage had been done. Just have the talk at a moment that is right.

How Is My Self-Esteem at This Time in My Life?

As we've already observed, many people in our society judge and value us based on our position. So when that position is gone, where's the value? Depending on your wiring, this may be a big issue or no issue at all. We have friends who love doing chores around the house and hanging out with their grandchildren, and find that is all they aspire to in their retirement years. They don't struggle with personal value and self-esteem. I, Hans, recently met a couple in their fifties who spend most of their time touring the country in their massive RV and seem to love it. They sold their business and love roaming the country with no thought of waning self-esteem.

But many of us do struggle with self-esteem issues because of our personalities. Rick and I are "driven" personalities, with an enormous need to make a difference with our lives. We have to be involved with things that have great meaning and purpose. Our lives need to continue to count and have significance. So for people wired like we are, there is a quest to find that new self-esteem and value in our encore.

Where Will I Find Creative Outlets to Make the Contributions I Still Want to Make?

Our desire is that you find a creative outlet that will give you meaning and purpose, as did my new friend at the grocery store who found his at Trader Joe's. But no matter what your outlet, one thing is certain: *you have to look for it.* Generally, the opportunities will not come to your door. This is a time to seek, to knock, to experiment, and to investigate. This is a time when we might consider taking classes at our community center or community college. I, Hans, wanted to learn how to become a podcaster as part of my new career of teaching on leadership, and I took an intensive month-long course and learned all the new skills related to podcasting on iTunes (check out the Leadership Answerman podcast). There are so many outlets waiting for the person willing to search.

What Lifestyle Changes Do I Need to Make Based on My Changing Medical Situation?

This issue is closely associated with where you will live. Senior living is an exploding industry in our country. Elder care and long-term care insurance is growing by leaps and bounds with the aging boomer population. We will have to make changes based on our medical situation, if our bodies and minds are beginning to give out on us. It's not a good idea to wait until a crisis hits to make lifestyle changes. Many of us are dealing with these very realities as we are caring for our elderly parents. The more decisions we can make about our own lifestyle situation now, the less we'll have to leave up to our children to make for us.

It's Never Too Late for Success

To finish this chapter, we want to share some success stories of people who accomplished their greatest life achievements during the years of the 60–80 Window. These are all well-known people, and that is why we are using them as examples. Most of us will not have their prominence, but there are great lessons to be learned from them as we write our own story.

People who have reached any significant level of success agree there are a few things successful people have in common: desire, determination, and a spirit that never gives up.

Ray Kroc.[5] At age fifty-two, Ray Kroc had suffered for years from arthritis and diabetes. Although Ray had poor health, and his bladder and most of his thyroid had been removed, he never stopped believing in himself and his biggest idea. It led to the start of McDonald's in 1955. By 1961, 228 McDonald's restaurants had been established and sales had reached $37 million. When Ray passed away in 1984 at age eighty-one, there were 7,500 McDonald's outlets around the world, and the number of outlets and sales is still growing. Ray Kroc was described as a simple man with a simple plan:

1. Never give up.
2. Always persevere.
3. Don't forget part 1 of the plan.

Alan Mulally. At age sixty-three, he took over the ailing Ford Motor Company in 2006. As of this writing he is in his late sixties and has led the company to new heights as the CEO of Ford. And along the way he has learned a lot of new tricks, having come from the airline industry, where he worked for Boeing in charge of the development of the Boeing 777.

Clint Eastwood. At age eighty and beyond, he is making some of his best, even Oscar-winning, movies. If you observe his body of work, it appears that his seventies and eighties are truly an amazing encore. "As we grow older," he says, "we must discipline ourselves to continue expanding, broadening, learning, keeping our minds active and open."[6]

Grandma Moses. She began painting at age seventy-six, after arthritis forced her to give up embroidery. She continued painting until 101.

Laura Ingalls Wilder. She published the first book in the Little House on the Prairie series at age sixty-five.

Benjamin Franklin. At age seventy, in 1776, he played an instrumental role in drafting and signing the Declaration of Independence. At eighty-one he signed the Constitution for the United States of America. That is what we would call meaning and purpose in your 60–80 Window!

Ronald Reagan. He became a governor of California at age sixty-one, after his career in Hollywood, and later served as the oldest sitting United States president, elected at age sixty-nine and serving until he was seventy-seven.

Colonel Sanders. The founder of Kentucky Fried Chicken was turned down over a thousand times when he tried to interest others in his recipe for chicken. He drove from town to town, often sleeping in his car, calling on restaurant owners. He strongly believed that the secret recipe would eventually pay off. His persistence and belief in himself and his recipe finally did pay off—in a big way! His tenacity is inspiring, especially when you consider that he found his success when he was sixty-five years of age. By 1976, Colonel Sanders was ranked the world's second most recognized celebrity by an independent survey. And in 1980, at the age of ninety, he traveled 250,000 miles a year visiting Kentucky Fried Chicken restaurants across the world before he was seriously slowed down by leukemia.

Colonel Sanders kept his chicken recipe a secret, but he was willing to share his recipe for success:

1. Never quit.
2. Always believe in yourself.
3. Be patient.
4. Be positive.

Nelson Mandela. As we are writing these pages, the world is mourning the death of this great world leader. The stunning thing to realize is that he was seventy-two years of age when he was released after twenty-six years in prison. He was elected to the presidency of South Africa two years later, at age seventy-four, and served for five years. Then he enjoyed another decade of prominence and influence before his health forced a full retirement.

———————

There are countless stories of people from all walks of life who achieved remarkable success in their encore years. The same types of characteristics can usually be found in almost every story about success. Being patient and persistent, having a positive attitude, and never giving up are the traits that are essential for success at any stage of life, especially in the 60–80 Window.

Reinventing Yourself
10 Lessons from Gandalf

We've always been fascinated by what we learn from and how we identify with characters from stories, novels, and movies. Perhaps we are not always sure that we get out of the story what the author intended, but we do get a picture of "what could be" in different situations in life. Reading books and watching movies are a lot like viewing art: each person gets out of a picture what they, influenced by their own experiences, see—their own interpretation. That's what happened to me, Rick, in reading and watching *The Hobbit* and the Lord of the Rings series by J. R. R. Tolkien.

In movies and books we connect with different characters of the plot depending on our own wiring. In *The Hobbit* and the Lord of the Rings, many would identify with Bilbo Baggins or Frodo. Some of you type-A leaders might well relate to Aragorn the king. But I didn't. I seemed to latch on to Gandalf—Gandalf the Grey, at the beginning. There is a great lesson here related to your encore. In case you don't remember the storyline or haven't seen the movies or read the books, here's a quick review.

In *The Hobbit*, Gandalf the Grey, a wizard, tricked Bilbo Baggins, a hobbit, into being a part of a great adventure to reclaim the dwarf kingdom of Erebor and the treasures that were guarded by the dragon Smaug. Bilbo reluctantly left the Shire to join a band of dwarfs to carry out this adventure. In the process, Bilbo encountered Gollum, a very strange cave creature, and obtained his powerful ring. Bilbo and his companions continued on, using the power of the ring and their own courage to defeat Smaug and restore the dwarfs' kingdom.

The Lord of the Rings series took place years later. Since Bilbo Baggins was too old to participate in this adventure, the cause fell to his nephew, Frodo. The ring was passed from Bilbo to Frodo to take to its final destination. In order to accomplish this, the Fellowship of the Ring was created, consisting of four hobbits, an elf, a dwarf, two humans, and a wizard. The ultimate goal was to have Frodo destroy the ring in the fires of Mount Doom to save the Shire and, in fact, all of Middle Earth. Mission accomplished.

What was an epiphany for me in following this story was the role of the wizard, Gandalf the Grey, and how he changed, even reinvented himself, as he became Gandalf the White. Gandalf the Grey was very much in charge when we first meet him in *The Hobbit*, laying out his plan for Bilbo, and later for Frodo, to start on their respective journeys. He was in control—direct and very strategic. He made sure everyone was in place to fulfill his or her roles.

In a battle to protect the Fellowship, Gandalf the Grey fought against Balrog. The powerful demon, sent from the first dark world, was dragged, fighting Gandalf, down into the dark pit inside the mountain of Moria. Gandalf sacrificed himself to allow his comrades to escape, and all thought he was dead, but later he returned as Gandalf the White.

Gandalf came back as a very different kind of wizard, still with a strong resolve to complete his task and life's work but with a very different approach. *He went from command and control to being more of a guiding light and encourager.* He didn't continue on with the Fellowship in their journey, but showed up when he was needed. He left much of the decision making to Frodo and the Fellowship. He knew what needed to happen, but left the actions and results to those involved in the plot. In the end, Frodo and the Fellowship accomplished their task of destroying the ring and bringing safety and harmony back to their world.

Here is the lesson I learned from Gandalf: as we get older, our role as it relates to those around us needs to change. We find that we shift from command and control to more of a place of influence. The idea of becoming an advisor, a mentor, or even a coach comes into play. It seemed to work for Gandalf the White, which opened up the door of my mind to consider how it could work for me and started me on a path that ushered me into what we have referred to as the elderlescence stage of life. Around that time I stepped down as president of OM USA, a command and control kind of position. I took on a higher-level job as the North American Area leader, which is an advisor-driven, mentor-oriented, counselor-focused role. I must say it was difficult to change from leading by power and authority to leading by influence. I had more influence but less direct control. It really was a struggle to make this change, but it was the beginning of my next journey of reinventing myself.

A real-life account of someone who reinvented himself is that of famous runner Jim Ryun. Jim had a storied track career with a number of unbelievable accomplishments. He was the first high school student to break the four-minute mile. He had world records in the 880-yard run and the 1500-meter run, two world records in the mile, and another world record in the indoor mile. In 1966 and 1967 he was the track and field athlete of the year, and in 1966, the *Sports Illustrated* "Sportsman of the Year." Also in 1966 he was ABC's *Wide World of Sports* "Athlete of the Year," along with many, many more accomplishments, including competing in three different Olympics.

With all of Jim's success, perhaps his most defining moment was a time of defeat. In 1972, Jim was running a qualifying heat in the Munich Olympics. He was tripped and fell, and later it was acknowledged that he was fouled. But, contrary to Olympic policy, he was not allowed to continue in the competition. He was the leading 1500-meter runner in the world at that time and was assured of a win—but missed out.

Many saw this as a failure on Jim's part, but what Jim learned through that perceived failure enhanced the rest of his life and helped him in the process of reinventing himself. Years later I, Rick, had the opportunity to spend some time with Jim, and I asked him about what he had learned in Munich. He told me that all of his life he had been a runner—first in all of his athletic endeavors. Quite frankly, not many could relate to him as a person due to his previous overwhelming success. When his failure to win gold in Munich occurred, people began to look at Jim differently. After that, Jim told me, people would walk up to him and begin to express their sorrow to him, saying, "The same thing that happened to you in Munich happened to me. I was fouled out in life at my job," or "My wife left me and it shouldn't have happened that way." People who felt they had also been treated unfairly in life began to relate to Jim in a completely different way. People could relate to Jim's failure much more than his success. It made him more accessible to people—more relatable.

After Jim's athletic career was over, he went on to become a member of the US House of Representatives for the state of Kansas. I can't help but think that Jim's perceived failure in obtaining the gold medal in Munich may have helped him reinvent himself into being a servant of the people.

Life is not always fair. Many times we face setbacks that throw us for a loop as we face great disappointment. For Gandalf, it was being taken down by Balrog and cast into the dark pit of Mount Moria. No one thought that would ever happen, but it did. For Jim Ryun, it was being unfairly fouled out of the 1500-meter race in the Olympics. In both cases we see a tragedy turned into triumph as they reinvented themselves. What they thought was the end was just an open door to a new beginning.

Can You Relate to a Teacher?

OK, perhaps you cannot relate to Gandalf or Jim Ryun. But who can't relate to a schoolteacher? We have not all been one, but we all know teachers and respect their role in our world. Cathey had a successful career as an agriculture teacher in her local elementary and middle schools. In her midfifties, God made it clear to her that it was time for her to retire. She sensed a very strong impression in her heart of hearts that she was to make a big change in her life. Those kinds of impressions are hard to explain, but if you have experienced it you understand what Cathey was feeling. She struggled with it for two years, but finally retired from her teaching career. Her husband was still gainfully employed, so she wondered what she was now to do, and what she could get involved in locally that would bring meaning and purpose to her life.

When Cathey finally retired, she struggled with feelings of insignificance. She was in the "land between" we discuss in depth in chapter 18. God impressed upon her that this was a season to focus on *being* rather than *doing*. Within a few months of listening for leading she was introduced to a method of farming called Farming God's Way, a project that helped people in undeveloped countries of the world develop better farming methods. She dove in and began to get involved. *The lesson here is that exploration is a huge part of launching your encore.* One thing leads to the next, and eventually lands you at a great new place of meaning and purpose.

During her involvement with Farming God's Way, Cathey had a chance to travel to various African countries. At this time she became very aware of the plight of oppressed women around the world. Additionally, around this time a speaker at Forest Home Conference Center challenged her with the idea of putting her faith ahead of her fears. She decided that her greatest fear was the fear of heights, so she began doing hard things specific to overcoming that fear. Her culminating activity was to climb Mount Whitney. On her way down the mountain, she asked God what she was to learn from all this. *What is this about, and what do you have for me in the future?*

As she descended the mountain she had a clear vision that her next mountain would be Mount Kilimanjaro, and she would climb with women from around the world for women and children around the world. Her purpose was to bring awareness to the plight of oppressed women and children around the world. Eventually this led to the creation of the "Freedom Climb," where forty-eight women from ten countries ascended Kilimanjaro to bring attention to the plight of oppressed, exploited, trafficked, and enslaved women and children. In the process they raised almost half a million dollars for these needy women with this first of many climbs that are continuing to occur around the world.

The best takeaway from Cathey's story is that she acted on her impressions and guidance from God as she sensed it was time to reinvent herself. As fearful as it can be, make the change. When we act, things begin to happen around us that are amazing and unexplainable. *You can't see the horizon if you are stuck in a deep rut.*

PART 3

The Stories

People Who Show Us the Way

Every generation thinks they are special. Many of us entering this later-life journey may feel as though no one has gone down this road before us. We boomers always have to do things differently. But are there any role models we would like to imitate? While this is a new journey for everyone who enters it, others have successfully gone before us. In these following pages we tell the stories of men and women we know who have walked this road well, and reinvented themselves with new meaning and purpose as they launched their encore.

Jane and Peggy Thayer, in the book *Elderescence: The Gift of Longevity*, observe that, "Longevity, once the gift of a few, has become the destiny of many."[1] As we noted earlier, by 2050 one in five Americans will be older than sixty-five. This 60–80 Window presents a couple of critical decades for tens of millions of boomers to deal with. Can we choose to contribute to society in productive ways? Are there people who can show us the way?

Nothing tells a truth better that real-life stories. We purposely chose stories of people from various positions and careers in life. Some were leaders and others were average working people who made the adjustments to live a great encore after their main act was over.

Couples Find Their Encore Together

11 Daryl and Karen Poppen

As married couples live life together they will encounter their encore years together, so planning what that will look like as a couple is important. Whether both have careers or only one is actually retiring from employment, there are still choices that they both need to make. Each spouse's career milestones affect the other spouse in huge ways. There must be a partnership as they figure out how they will fill their time and find meaning and purpose when one or both of them stop working.

Daryl and Karen Poppen were very intentional about planning for their encore. With the help of a conference, a recommended book, and some good advice, they made a plan ten years before they planned to retire and stuck with that plan, which resulted in a successful transition into their new lives. Now at age sixty-four, with one year of retirement under their belt, they recount the preparations they made together:

> At a Finishers Project Conference in 2002, we were encouraged to read the book *Halftime* by Bob Buford. Bob wants

people who are in the middle of their lives—their personal halftime—to think about what they want their second half to look like. Many people retire to play golf, travel, and do the things they want to do. He challenged us to look at retiring to serve others and to serve God. We had been building up treasure on earth during our first half, and he encouraged us to look at building up treasure in heaven in our second half. Since supporting missions had always been something we had done, we began to look at how the Lord might use us for missions in retirement.

We knew we had to do some things to prepare. One of the tasks Finishers recommended was to get our financial house in order, eliminate all debt, and make sure that we had the resources to carry out our plan. God has richly blessed us, and over the course of the next ten years we were able to do it. We worked and saved for a very long time and now have very good pensions so we are free to do what God calls us to do. A year ago we retired from our jobs in California and moved to Huntersville, North Carolina, because our son Doug, his wife, Jenn, and their three wonderful kids live here. We purposefully bought a house near them three years before retirement, and rented it out in preparation for our move there after we retired.

The Poppens each left meaningful careers—Karen had worked her way up through the school system, and during her last five years of employment she served as superintendent for a small rural school district in central California. It was a challenging time for the school district due to the economic crisis the state of California was going through, and she ended up having to delay her retirement a year to help with the transition to the new superintendent.

Daryl had previously held CFO positions at various schools and at Forest Home Christian Conference Center, and at the time of retirement was working the favorite job of his career as both administrator and small-group coordinator at New Life Christian Church in Turlock, California. As he looked at retirement, he knew he wanted to follow the advice he had received from Dr. Dick Hillis, the founder of Overseas Crusades, back in 1967: to do things that make a difference in the lives of others. Daryl said, "I haven't always done that as well as I would have liked, but I am excited about the journey we are on right now."

So what does that present journey through their encore look like? "I love to help others in many different ways," explained Daryl. "I help down at our church by leading a team of volunteers who help the staff with various facility setups. I also work with my son as he heads up a moving ministry to help various members and friends of the church when moving their residence is needed. We have also gone on a short-term mission trip to Long Island, Bahamas, and plan to go on several more mission trips in the future. Being around my son and his family brings me great joy. I *love* teasing and playing with our grandkids. I also enjoy the Bible studies I am in and the new friends we are making through our church."

Karen explained what they did to intentionally transition into new ways of spending their time in their new lives:

We arrived in North Carolina on October 1, 2012. We attended the church where our son and his family were attending and serving. We had visited there many times, so we knew that is where we wanted to attend, serve, and make friends. We sought out a home Bible study group as a couple, and we both began attending men's and women's studies. My husband connected with a group to play golf through someone in his men's study and began playing with them twice a week very soon after our arrival. I started participating in a tutoring program connected to our church at a local elementary school in January. Through our first year, we continued to volunteer in various areas at our church and take advantage of volunteer opportunities with Operation Mobilization, a mission organization we had supported over the years. We went on our first mission trip with our church in August 2013, and found it so fulfilling that we plan to do multiple trips each year. By the end of our first year, we were well connected with friends and participating in meaningful activities.

We find meaning and purpose through serving others and opening our home to share hospitality. Now that I'm retired, I have time to host various groups in our home, like Bible studies and book clubs, which is something I didn't have a lot of time for when I was working. I enjoy cooking for them and sharing our home as a peaceful oasis in the chaos of life. I have also worked to form relationships with several neighbors and had them over for lunch.

Successful encores as a couple take planning as a couple, and here are some words of advice that Daryl and Karen give:

- Think ahead about what you want your retirement to look like. Begin praying about and planning for this transition at least ten years before you expect to retire.
- Set yearly goals so that at the end of ten years you are where you want to be, financially and in every other way. For example, we set a goal of being debt-free when we retired, so we kept this goal in mind when making purchases.
- Be open to what God has for you. It may not be what you had envisioned, but be open to God's direction. His ways are always better than our ways.
- Begin to pray about what you want your retirement to look like and expose yourself to different missions opportunities that may be available to you.

A Professional Finds a Second Chance

12 Julie Clark

Even pilots need to find an encore. With the current retirement age for commercial pilots locked in at age sixty-five, many productive professionals in this industry find themselves dropped in the middle of a satisfying career. No longer able to work for the airlines, many pilots struggle in their personal lives at this point.

Enter the story of Julie Clark, who created a different path for herself as a commercial airline pilot. This is an amazing story of a woman who leveraged her love of flying into a hobby that became an encore career. Now in her seventies, Julie Clark continues to entertain spectators at airshows all across America and Canada. She shows us how to do what you love and love what you do after being forced to retire from a fulfilling career.

There was never a doubt that Julie Clark was born to fly. "While most eight-year-old girls were playing with dolls," explained Julie, "I was building models of airplanes and reading all I could about flying." Adding fuel to the fire that committed Julie to aviation was her father, Ernie Clark, a commercial airline pilot for Pacific Airlines. "My dad got me interested in flying," recalled Julie, with a smile. "I got really excited when he would take me along on airline flights in the DC-3 or F-27. Dad would put me into the baggage compartment and then, from inside the airplane, he would open the baggage bin and sneak me into the cockpit. I had to beg and plead, but I thought that was the greatest thing, when I could go fly with my dad."

Ironically, it was her father's fate that had a more profound effect on her. Ernie Clark flew in the 1960s, when cockpits were left unlocked during flight. In 1964, while Captain Clark was filling in for a pilot who had called in sick and was en route from Reno, Nevada, to Oakland, California, a passenger entered the unlocked cockpit with a gun and killed Captain Clark and his first officer. The airplane went down, killing all on board. "That incident," Julie explained, "brought about the law requiring cockpit doors to remain locked during commercial flights."

It was a difficult time for Julie, but her goal never changed. In fact, she became even more determined. In 1967, Julie spent her college book money on flying lessons. After college, years of working two or three jobs, and taking virtually any flying job to build time and higher ratings, Julie's major break came in 1976 when Golden West Airlines, a West Coast commuter airline, hired her to fly DeHavilland Twin Otters. The first and only woman ever to fly for Golden West, Julie flew mail at night and passengers till noon, in her continuing effort to build time. In 1977, when Hughes Airwest (formerly Pacific Airlines) hired Julie, she became one of the first women to fly for a major airline and started what became a storybook career. Hughes Airwest became Republic Airlines and then Northwest Airlines. Julie became a captain for Northwest Airlines in 1984. After a long and enjoyable career, Julie retired from Northwest Airlines in 2004 when she reached the milestone forced retirement age of sixty.

It was at this very juncture that our encore picks up. When Julie was forced into retirement, the mandatory age was sixty. The airline industry has since raised that retirement age for commercial pilots to sixty-five, and is considering going up to sixty-seven or sixty-eight. But for all those pilots who love to fly, this can be a very tough time of transition. Just the words "forced retirement" ring of a death sentence. Like many people, Julie did not want to retire. But it was forced upon her and she had choices to make. Here was a woman who broke the glass ceiling in commercial aviation and then one day was forced to stop doing the thing she loved the most.

How did she cope? Julie Clark has launched an encore that few people can dream of. Fortunately she had already laid the groundwork for her second career. Long before her retirement, Julie purchased an airplane, a Beechcraft T-34 Mentor, which became her hobby and side career. Restoration fans will appreciate that Julie bought her Beechcraft T-34 in 1977, "sight unseen" at a government surplus auction in Anchorage, Alaska, for $18,000. She flew the airplane, dubbed *Free Spirit*, 2,900 miles to her home in California. Julie personally and painstakingly restored the aluminum airplane, hand-polishing inside and out. "Over the next four years, I spent many long hours bringing the airplane back to mint condition," she said. She created her own airshow company and began performing in shows on the side when she was not performing her duties with the airline. Her airshow company became very successful as Julie pioneered new features of aerobatics that were unique and huge crowd-pleasers.

No woman likes to admit her age, but Julie was forced to retire at age sixty from the airlines in 2004, so you can do the math. She continues to fly today and wows spectators from coast to coast in her airshow performances. With over thirty years as a solo aerobatic airshow pilot, Julie has earned the admiration of fans everywhere and garnered many awards and honors. Julie is one of the few airshow greats to be featured in a biography; her amazing story is told in *Nothing Stood in Her Way*. It is the first such biography published by Women in Aviation International and tells of the amazing strengths and perseverance of this remarkable airshow star. Check out her website, www.julieclarkairshows.com, and go watch her fly at an airshow near you.[1]

Julie's story is a bit unusual because she built a thriving side career while she was working full-time in her main career. So she literally stepped off of one escalator onto a fast-moving second one that she continues to ride with great fulfillment. It never hurts to be thinking about and building our "Plan Bs" while we are still in our "Plan A" jobs.

What are the lessons for us all in this amazing journey of Julie Clark?

- Nothing comes easy in life—there was a lot of hard work in this encore story.
- Don't let heartache and disappointments steal your dreams.
- Prepare early for what you will do later.
- It never hurts to have a "Plan B" in your pocket to pull out when you need it.
- You can turn a hobby that you love into a new career—Julie is one of many people who have done just that.

Taking Advantage of a Rolling Retirement

13 Tom Zeulner

Some retirements, rather than being the complete ending of a career, can be more of a "rolling retirement" where you might continue to use your skills and experience in the same industry or even the same company you retired from, but in a different relationship with a different time commitment.

Tom Zeulner, technically a "retired" firefighter, has remained very active in the career he has enjoyed his whole adult life, but on his terms. He has configured his encore so that his limited work fits his family priorities and his desire to be involved in his community, while at the same time leaving the more dangerous and physically challenging activities of his profession to the younger firefighters.

For thirty-three years Tom served his community and the people in it through his career in the fire department. When he did retire, he was in upper management as battalion chief with the San Luis Obispo City Fire Department in California.

Tom first entered the fire service in 1975 at age nineteen, after working in banking and the retail grocery business. He had dreams of becoming a civil engineer. The fire service never crossed his mind until his girlfriend's neighbor asked him if he was interested in a job fighting wildland fires for the Los Angeles County Fire Department. He tested for the position and was accepted at the lowest rung on the ladder in the fire service. It was during this time with LA County Fire that he knew without a doubt God had placed him in the correct vocation for him and would bless his career in the fire service.

Ten months after he began his career, Tom was a full-time firefighter for the County of Santa Barbara, California. After serving in that department for three years, he joined the City of San Luis Obispo Fire Department. He and his wife, Jody, settled down in Atascadero where they had two sons and built two houses, and Tom was promoted up through the ranks of engineer, captain, and battalion chief.

Tom was still in his early fifties and enjoying his career . . . so what made him consider retirement?

Things were going great. Both my sons were married and working as pastors in churches in Orange County. My wife and I were new grandparents. I worked for an amazing fire chief at the time and loved going to work. I was still working shift work (24 hours on/24 hours off) and responding to emergencies daily. Firefighting is dangerous work and during the last few years of my career I witnessed firefighters falling through roofs and trapped by falling ceilings, and I did not want to lose a firefighter on my watch. I was the guy in charge at the fire scene.

Firefighting is also a physically demanding job, and after thiry-three years of firefighting, vehicle accidents, hazardous material spills, and medical calls my body (which I kept in good shape) was wearing out. I had bad knees, a bad back, and lungs that had breathed too much smoke. After witnessing many fellow firefighters retire past their prime with major health issues, I wanted to leave the job I loved while I could still be the husband, father, and grandfather that my family deserved. I could handle the aches and pains my body gave me, but the stress on my heart each and every time the alarm sounded worried me. I wanted to walk out of the job I loved with my head held high and not on a work-related injury or illness.

Firefighting is one of those careers that sets full retirement age earlier than most, due to the physical demands of the job. When Tom could see that "exit door" in the near future, he let his boss, the fire chief, know his plans. The chief countered with an offer of a new position for three to five years as a deputy fire chief, if he could get the position funded, which would mainly be office work with a normal schedule. It sounded like a great plan, but the downturn in the economy at that point didn't allow the funding of the position at that time. Tom went ahead and submitted retirement paperwork on his terms and timing. However, that did not end his relationship with the fire department.

Tom had been working on four major projects for the city fire department the previous few years as part of his duties as a battalion chief. Prior to Tom's official retirement, the fire chief asked him if he would consider coming back part-time to continue working on these large capital projects since he was the person who had the most information and background on them. And so, the week after he officially retired Tom began working twenty hours a week as a contract employee of the city on an eighteen-month contract.

How did Tom feel about this next stage of his life?

So my next steps were laid out before me and I could not have been any happier. I was able to set my own schedule, to be home at night, to travel to see my granddaughter, to volunteer at my church one day a week doing maintenance, and I was still associated with the fire department. God knew I had to be weaned away from the fire service a little at a time. That contract also allowed me to work as part of a federal fire management team on the large wildland fires that occur every year in the western states. Most of the type of work I do on these large fires is on a computer in fire camp and not out on the fire line . . . I leave that up to the younger firefighters.

The eighteen-month contract went well as a number of projects were reduced or completed. Tom was then offered a twelve-month contract for ten hours a week, which allowed him to take on another project, working with the fire chief to rewrite the city's emergency operations plan. At the end of that contract he had his final exit discussion with the fire chief, leaving the project 95 percent completed. The chief said he would complete it, but sadly, two months later the fire chief, at the age of sixty-one, had a major heart attack and passed away. Two months after his death the city manager called Tom and asked him to come back to work on a contract basis to finish the city's emergency operations plan because he was the one person who knew the most about it and could finish it.

Fast-forward now to present day. Tom is getting to the end of his fifties, and he still serves on a federal fire team and works about thirty days a year on large wildland fires. He still has plans to use his skills and experience in his sixties—desiring to be accepted as a member of a national FEMA response team and help during national emergencies or disasters.

What else brings Tom purpose and meaning after retirement and as part of his encore?

- More time for family, as he and Jody are free to help their kids and grandkids by babysitting and with home improvement projects once or twice a month.
- Time for volunteering at church—one day a week doing vehicle and building maintenance, serving on the deacon board, and, along with his wife, being a marriage mentor for struggling couples.
- Helping in the community through his church's "Love in Action" ministry, volunteering time, tools, trucks, and talent to help those who need something done at their house but don't have the means to pay for it.
- Being involved in international missions trips, including serving missionaries in Mexico who are supported by his church and participating in two trips to Haiti after the 2010 earthquake as part of the Firefighters for Christ emergency response team.

And finally, as we have asked with each of our encore stories, what advice would Tom give for those considering how to build their encore?

- Family first . . . when in doubt . . . family first.
- Be your spouse's best friend and have common interests.
- Volunteer: church, community, and missions.
- Work part-time—it keeps you sharp.
- Have fun.
- Take a little more time prior to making big decisions.

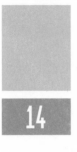

More Impact in Her Encore Years

Dorothy McCullough

Hindsight is always helpful when evaluating effectiveness of decisions and choices over time. Dorothy McCullough, now age ninety-one, was able to give us her perspective of how she has spent her encore years after her retirement at age sixty-eight from the role of assistant vice president for development at Harvey Mudd College of Science and Engineering in Claremont, California. She has been a lady of great influence, both during her career and in her encore, but her beginnings would not have predicted that.

Dorothy started her college education at the University of Oklahoma studying business, but she didn't do well in the midst of the engineers she was studying with. Because her aunt was a teacher at Woodbury University in Burbank, California, a four-year career school, she moved there to continue her studies. Then World War II happened and that, of course, changed everything. There were such good jobs being offered, and since during her three semesters of college education she had at least learned to type, she left school and took a secretarial job that started her on a career path that had nothing to do with any training she had been given! Dorothy's career spanned thirty years of work at Harvey Mudd University, serving under three college presidents. During the transition to the third president, she began to feel that the time for her retirement had come. The new president was bringing fresh ideas to Harvey Mudd, and he and she became good friends while working together to implement them. At one point he required that everyone on staff over the age of sixty-five retire, except for her, and she could stay as long as she wanted. (You could not get away with that kind of edict today!) But she still felt the time for retirement was right.

> I chose the timing because the office was changing so much at that time. I felt that what I had done in helping to build Harvey Mudd during my time there was complete. The computers had come in. There was a whole different technology in the office and I was not at the place to dive into that learning curve. At the age of sixty-eight I needed to be retired. I felt my work there was done.

Dorothy and her husband had been married for fifty years and had three children. At the time she retired she didn't know what her next years would hold. She belonged to organizations through Harvey Mudd, and even though she had retired they would not let her go. She was a member of some foundations, one of which was the ARCS (Achievement Rewards for College Scientists) Foundation, which had her travel throughout the United States representing science colleges. She also served with a group of women who were raising money for scholarships for science students, and they had great connections. Another woman was the wife of a Supreme Court Justice who had them into the court for dinner. Those are just a few examples of the circles Dorothy was a part of.

Dorothy found that being retired gave her freedom from conflicts of interest as she was raising funds for other schools, such as Cal Tech, since she was no longer working at Harvey Mudd. She could serve as a volunteer with this organization, and did so for about twenty years.

Other activities she filled her time with included international travel for pleasure and being active in her church. She started an auxiliary chapter for Forest Home Christian Conference Center in Claremont, and they met in her home for years. She was also a discussion leader for Women's Bible Study Fellowship. She also has greatly enjoyed having the time to be more involved with her family—children, grandchildren, and now great-grandchildren.

Dorothy was also one of the founders of Shoes That Fit, an organization that provides shoes for kids in need, and her involvement continued into her encore years. This part of her involvement started at Harvey Mudd, when a woman in financial aid had seen a boy whose feet had been turned under by shoes that were too small, and had said, "I've just got to do something for these kids." She started Shoes That Fit and went after Dorothy for help with fund-raising. Dorothy had just inherited some money, and used it to help turn this new initiative into a legitimate nonprofit. After her retirement, Dorothy continued with Shoes That Fit for a time, serving on the board and also as a coordinator. She would buy the shoes and take them down to a school to a nurse and say, "Please put these on this little boy; he needs to graduate."

Today Shoes That Fit is the main charity for Nordstrom's, has received many awards, and is all over the United States, but initially it was run out of Dorothy's garage. She would say that this was one of the transition things that just "fell in her lap." *Family Circle* magazine heard about it, interviewed the founder, and published a story about it. From that point on

Shoes That Fit exploded and they could no longer run it out of her garage. They called in Harvey Mudd students to get it organized and on computers. Dorothy told the founder that the time had come for a new board because their group was the hands-on people doing the work but they needed people who could technically run the organization. The establishment of the new board ended Dorothy's involvement and the founder eventually turned the organization over to new directors, but they have been gracious in keeping Dorothy informed of the status of the organization over the years.

Dorothy is now in her nineties, and when asked about how she has found meaning and purpose in her eighties, she responded:

> I had friends who were already in this retirement community where I now live who kept saying that I needed to move in there. I had stayed in my house for many years and I was beginning to look at it and say, "Well, maybe I need to have the floors redone, or put in a new heating system." And I said to myself, *No, I am not going to spend these years doing those types of things. I am going to enjoy life and be with people. I am not going to keep fixing up a house.*

After fifty years of marriage Dorothy had outlived her husband, as many aging women do. At the Mt. San Antonio Gardens retirement community where she moved, she found an unexpected but lovely turn of events in her life.

> At age eighty-one I married a wonderful Christian man and we had five years of just an incredible life. This marriage was an encouragement to people who had had difficulties finding the right person, and I had so many young people say, "You have really given us hope."
>
> His death was very difficult for me because it had been such a perfect time. In it, God gave me the opportunity to

renew, go back to the beginning of my faith and start over and to begin to come out of a lot of things that had been negative in my faith.

Even now, with some physical limitations that have come with age, Dorothy has found ways to be involved in her community.

I belong to a group at the Gardens, where I live, called the Bag Ladies. It was started by a group of women who liked to have lunch together, and they always invite two people who are brand-new to the community, to answer their questions about living there, and so forth. The only way to get into this group is when someone dies, so it took a while before I was finally asked to join, and I am currently the elder member of the group. Twice a month we have a luncheon in our homes that we prepare for the new people. You get to know the new people as they open up and share their life experiences. It is a lot of fun. You have to learn to keep moving. I also learned to play Bridge at that time, and I like that and other card games that we play.

What advice would Dorothy give to those in their fifties or sixties who are thinking about their encore?

- Don't be afraid of retirement and wonder what you are going to do. Opportunities will come to you that will keep you involved.
- Leave well, and don't burn the bridges behind you. Stay involved in ways that interest you.
- Keep involved in the community.
- Enjoy the extra time with your family.

Taking a Leap of Faith

15 Sam and Jenny Webster

S
am was a chemical engineer by training who worked for a large chemical company. When his division was acquired by another company and jobs were being eliminated and restructured, he and his wife, Jenny, read a useful book called *Halftime* by Bob Buford. During the upheaval in his working world, they realized they really needed to be thinking about "second half" issues. The couple was moved by what they read, so they went away for the weekend to reflect and ponder their future. During that weekend they read Buford's follow-up book, *Game Plan*, which included more practical and tactical life-planning tips.

Have you ever had a watershed moment like Sam and Jenny? Most of us have from time to time in our lives. That weekend they prayed, "God, what would you have us do next?" They spent time considering the future, looking at the past, seeing how God had gifted them and what passions he had given them. They wrote up a game plan that included moving to Atlanta, Georgia, for a new job that had been offered to Sam by the acquiring company. Although the plan they wrote up that weekend away had some additional bullet points they eventually wanted to pursue, they folded it up, put it into the book, and stuck it up on the shelf.

The Websters moved to Atlanta, where they worked for five more years. Sam had spent his thirty-year career in business leadership and technical management roles, and he loved his job. He kept right on working, though that plan tucked away in the *Game Plan* book was nudging at their subconscious minds. They could not forget what they had written and what they felt God had impressed on their hearts that weekend.

Their plan had suggested that, in 2009, they would change from full-time business to part-time business and part-time ministry, in an intentional way. But they didn't know how that was going to happen. Toward the end of 2008, a friend of theirs who was in ministry in China, and whom they had been supporting for thirty years, wrote to them and said, "If you ever want to come to China and hang out with students, I have a place for you to stay." Sam thought, *I would love to do that, but I don't know how to leave my busy job to go do it.* God works in mysterious ways! Just a few months later, when Sam was laid off at age fifty-two due to another acquisition, he realized the opportunity had arrived.

Sam and Jenny pulled the *Game Plan* book off of the shelf, and realized that five years previously they had decided that in 2009 they would do something very different—and here they were in 2009 with the freedom to pursue something new. He wrote to his friend in China and said, "I'm in! When can I come?" He didn't know how it was all going to fit together, but was willing to go and see what would happen. (Taking action and moving forward is always the best way to launch your encore.)

As Sam was preparing to go to China for a couple of weeks, he had a plan in mind. When he came back, he would look into several international opportunities that could be job options for him. Then he would lay them on the table before God, and ask him which to do. When he shared this plan with the pastor at his church, the pastor sat back and said, "Do you want to make God laugh?" "What do you mean?" asked Sam. "That is not how you deal with the Creator of the universe," the pastor answered. "You don't give the Creator three options and constrain him. What you should do is pray and ask God to put one thing on the table, and then ask him for the courage to obey."

Sam thought that advice sounded very spiritual, but he didn't know how to do what his pastor suggested. *How does that really work in real life?* he thought. And so he walked away that day a bit confused, but figured he would keep pursuing his new dream. Before long Sam was in China for a couple of weeks, and strange and amazing doors began to open. The friend he was visiting in China spent a lot of time at a local Chinese university. That university noticed Sam had a strong business background. They asked him to give some business lectures during the week while he was visiting, which he was happy to do. They set up a different business talk every day at different universities, so he prepared and gave the lectures.

At the end of his visit the president of one of the universities asked him to consider moving to China to become an international trade teacher. That was not on Sam's radar! He had no idea this might happen. Before he went to China he had prayed, "God, if you have something for us in China that is longer term, open those doors clearly." But when the offer came, it shocked him! He told the president he had to go home and talk to his wife about it.

Sam and Jenny prayed and talked about it for a while, but still had some reservations. Sam started to do a job search at home in the United States—doing research, filling out applications, having interviews. Over the months it turned out there was only one job being offered: the teaching job in China! They kept waiting and waiting and decided that if, at the end of August, they still didn't have another job offer, they would have to consider that this was the plan for them, and sure enough, at the end of August it was still the only offer.

Looking at this story from God's point of view, there was a lot of waiting for Sam and Jenny to finally give in to the obvious. As an engineer, Sam went to his spreadsheets where he kept the records of his job search and saw that he had made one hundred job contacts and had had many interviews all the way to the very end . . . and then nothing. So Sam and Jenny finally believed that God wanted them to go, and decided to take the job in China. Then, true to form for what often happens, in the next few weeks he received many job offers from different places that all seemed like the perfect job . . . and they felt like God was asking them, *Are you serious about taking the job I led you to?* As they continued on with the process, in obedience, through many confirmations it became more and more clear that this was God's plan for them.

This is a great story of patience and plodding. We love that, because that is a lot of what launching your encore is all about. Rarely is the decision about what to do next a slam dunk. During an exploratory visit to China, Sam and Jenny realized just how hard this new life was going to be, but still moved forward in their preparations. It is one thing to visit a foreign country for a few weeks as a tourist and quite another to actually move there. When they decided they were going to move for sure, their next priority became recruiting a prayer support team to help them survive what they knew would be very hard, if not impossible!

As of this writing Sam and Jenny have been living in China for five years and their encore move has been a smashing success. They have had a large group back home praying for them, and have kept them informed with weekly emails throughout the years they have been in China. As they shared their story with us, they wanted us to let our readers know that they feel it is impossible to survive without the support of their prayer team. It never gets easier!

Before we get to some lessons drawn from the story of the Websters, we want to give you some insight into the challenges they continue to face living in a foreign country. In China nothing made sense to them and they found it hard to "make things happen," so Sam felt he was just left to trust in God and watch him show up and work. This lack of clarity and planning was a challenge for Sam, who was trained as an engineer to plan, design, deliver, and measure.

There was a lot of fear that first year caused by living in a country so different from what they were used to. Not only was this not America, but for the first time they were living in a place with restrictions and a very different political system. Over time the fear has diminished and they have seen many amazing things that God has allowed them to be a part of.

Meaning and purpose come to Sam and Jenny when they see changed lives as a result of being there and just being available to interact and share with students as they have opportunity. Their joy comes from seeing what God chooses to do and lets them participate in.

This is how Sam feels today: "I really enjoyed my job before I came to do this, but now that I have experienced what we are doing here in China, I could never go back to the old job." People who know Sam and Jenny say that they have never seen them so energized about life and their future. If you sit down with Sam he will talk your ear off in his exuberance for their newfound encore. Sam had several words of advice for people who might be thinking of a similar type of encore.

Don't let false barriers stop you.

Previously Sam had thought that maybe when they were in their sixties they would do this. He didn't know at the time that in China you can't be a university teacher after age sixty, but God knew. Sam has seen good friends think they might want to do something similar. But they get to be in their late fifties and for one reason or another barriers rise up to keep them from actually going. "I am so thankful that God interrupted our lives," said Sam, "because we probably would not have chosen this. If you think this is in your future, don't wait. Start now. Don't miss it."

Don't let fear about finances stop you.

Sam believes that as people get older, they get stuck in the security trap of thinking they need to keep working and store up more money, especially when faced with a jittery economy. "When we examined our savings and cash flow, we decided that we could stay in China until age sixty-five before running out of money," said Sam. "But we have seen through various circumstances that all we have spent has been replenished, and we are in good shape." If you think that God wants you to do something now, don't wait until you have "enough" money.

Beware of the expectation gap.

Jenny has always been a wonderful homemaker, managing the house (and making lists to help Sam remember what he needs to do). But when they went to China, she worried that people would expect her to instantly become a different person, the kind that you read about in missionary biographies. Regardless of their validity, those perceived expectations can create fear and stress, leading to depression and doubt. During their five years in China, Sam and Jenny have found that their love for each other and for their students opens more doors for ministry than any programs and strategies found in a book. There seems to be an unlimited number of opportunities to serve God when you enter a crosscultural role. They both work hard to stay focused on what they believe God has called them to do and to be, saying no (verbally and in their hearts) to things that are outside of that zone. When fears arise due to an "expectation gap," they focus on pleasing God, not men. While God will stretch them, he will not expect them to be someone other than who he made them to be.

Learn to work as a team if you are married.

As a couple, it is important to understand each other's differences and capacities. Sam, an extrovert, can handle way more social engagements than his wife, and he has learned to manage that to protect Jenny from getting overly stressed to a point that she is not able to thrive or even endure in the situation. Sometimes this has meant hard choices when it seemed like great opportunities had to be turned down, but it has been very important for them to understand their limits. They have also used these boundaries to communicate a good example of how to keep a marriage strong to the students they are working with.

PART 4

The Plan

Finding Your Meaning and Purpose

Yogi Berra often said, "When you come to a fork in the road, take it!"[1] We hope that by now you are convinced that staying on autopilot is not a good aging strategy. It's time for concrete solutions for the possible paths we can choose as we seek to contribute in this life stage. These pages lay out, in specifics, the road map for finding meaning and purpose in the 60–80 Window. Most of us will retire three or more times in our lifetime. There will be a rolling retirement picture for many of us.

How will we make this work? We have shared some great stories, and now it's time for you to take some steps to launch your encore—or to keep at it if you have already begun. In order to succeed in this 60–80 Window, you may need to learn some new life skills to navigate the future.

Your final act really can be your greatest. This life stage has the potential to be one of your finest. This final section is packed full of great tools, options, and "how-tos" to make that happen. Join us on the journey as we seek to find meaning and purpose after moving beyond fulfilling, full-time careers.

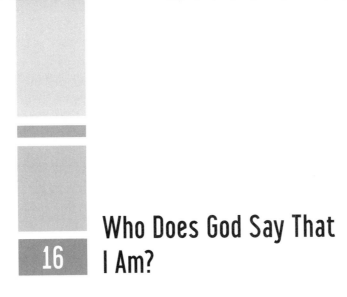

Who Does God Say That I Am?

16

Perhaps we should start this chapter with a disclaimer. We both recognize that people of many different worldviews will read our book. At least we hope so! Some of you are people of faith, others not. We approached our assignment in writing this book with the commitment that we would offer our thoughts to a wide-ranging audience. If you are a follower of Christ, you will especially appreciate some of our spiritual references and biblical observations. But if you're not a follower of our faith, we do respect you and know that you can get a lot out of our teaching anyway. In this chapter we will explore what we believe is God's view of old age. If that doesn't particularly interest you, feel free to move on to the next chapter. We won't be offended. Or, better yet, read on—you just might be surprised at the value of this chapter.

Our message in this chapter is this: *God doesn't give up on us when we get old.* In fact, the opposite is true, as we see the honor given to elders in the Bible. Let's consider God's view of us in this later-life stage of the 60–80 Window. We have already talked about the danger of making our positions and careers define us. In God's view, *who we are is more important than what we do.* More than ever, at this later time in our lives, followers of Jesus need to center on their identity in Christ, not their job, position, role, or authority.

I, Hans, and my wife, Donna, have four wonderful children. We feel so blessed to watch them grow as adults. They're getting married and producing lots of their own children as the next generation emerges. By the way, we think that grandchildren are a gift from God that softens the blow of old age. We have three sons and one daughter. Our daughter, Cambria, decided to get tattoos not long after she went away to college. We weren't supportive of the idea, but ultimately we did not stand in her way and forbid it. For some of you reading this, you probably would have seen it differently and you would have forbidden her. Her first tattoo reads, "Psalm 139." She chose that as a proclamation and a personal reminder of God's great love for her and how He made her. The essence of Psalm 139 is that *we are fearfully and wonderfully made.* This passage has always been a deep encouragement to me when I get down on myself. The Bible teaches in this psalm that we are each a stunning trophy of God's creation—inside and out. That promise goes for every one of us. Yes, Cambria went on to get some other tattoos. All of them are beautiful and have deep meaning. For her generation, tattoos are a way to communicate their values on their bodies. She tells me that, "We don't only use them just to communicate to others what we care about but also as a way of remembering where we came from and what we love."

There is no greater passage of Scripture to lock in our identity before God than Psalm 139 and, in keeping with her tattoo, Cambria has memorized it. Today she is newly married with a vibrant faith and ministry alongside her husband, Max. Her passion is to serve her Lord Jesus, and

Donna and I are so proud of the woman she has grown to be. A faithful, gifted, and artistic servant of Jesus, Cambria is living in Cape Town, South Africa, where she and Max reach out to the poorest of the poor on this planet in the name of Jesus.

God never changes his view of us from day to day, but our employers do . . . our co-workers do . . . our family does. In fact, many of us may struggle with our own view of ourselves from day to day. It is a great anchor for our persona to know that God is pleased with who we are from our birth to our death, in every stage of our life. In Psalm 139:13–14 we read, "For you created my inmost being; you knit me together in my mother's womb. I praise you because I am fearfully and wonderfully made; your works are wonderful, I know that full well." Does that reality diminish as we grow older? No, we are wonderfully made for the elder season of our lives just as much as when we were thriving teenagers. If God were in charge of billboards, magazine covers, and advertising, we would see a lot more older faces!

Let's explore some of the great comments in the Bible about getting older—we will start with a couple of my favorites since I, Hans, started growing gray even before my forties.

> Gray hair is a crown of splendor;
> it is attained in the way of righteousness.
> (Prov. 16:31)

> The glory of young men is their strength,
> gray hair the splendor of the old. (20:29)

Insight: the energy of any society is with the youth. But the crowning achievement in life is to actually grow old with dignity and have that place of elder honor.

> Is not wisdom found among the aged?
> Does not long life bring understanding? (Job 12:12)

Insight: here is what God says is the role elders play in our world. They are the ones who have the wisdom and understanding the younger generations need. Wouldn't it be refreshing if our culture actually sought out and listened to its elders?

> Do not cast me away when I am old;
>> do not forsake me when my strength is gone.
> (Ps. 71:9)

Insight: the writer of this psalm expresses what we all fear, that we will be abandoned and alone in our senior years. He is pleading with God not to forget him when his strength is gone and he is no longer useful in society. It seems clear from the full body of what we know about God in the Bible that he is not going to forget us at that stage of our lives.

> Since my youth, God, you have taught me,
>> and to this day I declare your marvelous deeds.
> Even when I am old and gray,
>> do not forsake me, my God,
> till I declare your power to the next generation,
>> your mighty acts to all who are to come.
> (vv. 17–18)

Insight: here we have the same fear expressed as earlier in the same psalm. The repetition of ideas in the poetry of the psalms is a common literary technique. There is repetition and then the building of a new idea. The writer adds here the role he wants to play in his old age: that of communicator of God's mighty power. Those of us who have walked with God for many decades can tell the young people about all God has done for us. We have seen the faithfulness of God displayed time and again! This really is what our book is all about: giving back from a life fully blessed.

> Stand up in the presence of the aged, show respect for the elderly and revere your God. I am the LORD. (Lev. 19:32)

Insight: we love this one! Right out of the mouth of God in his instructions to Moses: stand up with respect when older people enter your space. Wow, would that be interesting! Here is that critical word *respect*—the younger are to give the older a place of reverence and respect. Unfortunately, for many of us as we grow older, we feel that our society pushes us to the sidelines and we "can't get no respect." It is always refreshing to run into young people who do respect their elders and make that plainly known to us.

> He died at a good old age, having enjoyed long life, wealth and honor. His son Solomon succeeded him as king. (1 Chron. 29:28)

Insight: this was the death of David, who lived to be an old man and died with great dignity.

> And so Job died, an old man and full of years. (Job 42:17)

Insight: both of these previous two passages, referring to David and Job, remind us of the wisdom of Abraham Lincoln, who said, "And in the end, it's not the years in your life that count. It's the life in your years."[1] These great men had a lot of life in their years and died full of dignity.

> Moses was a hundred and twenty years old when he died, yet his eyes were not weak nor his strength gone. The Israelites

grieved for Moses in the plains of Moab thirty days, until the time of weeping and mourning was over. (Deut. 34:7–8)

Insight: Moses lived well and finished well. When his career was over, he was still physically and mentally sharp, as we can read in these verses. He died full of dignity with his honor in place. God must have been so pleased with that life full of obedience and a faith that never wavered.

Teach the older men to be temperate, worthy of respect, self-controlled, and sound in faith, in love and in endurance.
Likewise, teach the older women to be reverent in the way they live, not to be slanderers or addicted to much wine, but to teach what is good. (Titus 2:2–3)

Insight: Harriet Beecher Stowe said, "So much has been said and sung of beautiful young girls, why doesn't somebody wake up to the beauty of old women?"[2] That pretty well sums up what we, the authors, think of older women. They have a great place in our society and our churches to teach right living to those who are coming up behind them. You met two such wonderful older ladies in part 3 of our book, Dorothy and Julie.

And finally, we finish this chapter with our favorite passage showing what God thinks of us as we age into our elderlescence years.

Even to your old age and gray hairs
I am he, I am he who will *sustain you*.
I have made you and I will *carry you*;
I will sustain you and I will *rescue you*. (Isa. 46:4, emphasis added)

Insight: here is a promise from God you can cling to until your life is over. This verse from Isaiah is well worth memorizing if you are over sixty. When we are old and our hair is gray, God will do three things for us: sustain us, carry us, and rescue us if we need it.

What can we conclude about God's view of old age? It seems pretty countercultural to our Western view. Our Western culture honors youth; the Bible honors old age. We fixate on the young and tend to want to put the old people out to pasture. The Bible says the older generations need to be around and we need to listen to them. We in our society want to relegate the growing population of older Americans to senior centers, retirement homes, and 55+ communities. Not surprising, here is another place where culture and the Bible clash.

Our biggest issue with how our society treats the older generations is this idea of segregation. We would argue that the best solution is to keep the generations together as long as possible. It makes for the best communities, the best companies, and the best churches. That community, organization, cause, company, or church that consists only of people under forty definitely lacks the dimension the Bible teaches is critically important: the intermingling of all generations.

Who does the Bible say I am, as I am getting older? The key word from Scripture is the word *respect*. There is a place for great respect for old age in the Bible. Old age is to be honored and revered. And the wisdom and knowledge of older people are to be sought out and gleaned by the younger generations.

The Toolbox

17
Who Do I Want to Become Next?

Jim was a good friend who asked me, Rick, to give him and his whole family the DiSC Personality Style Assessment. In the DiSC acronym, "D" is *dominance*; direct, strong-willed, and forceful. "I" stands for *influence*; sociable, talkative, and lively. "S" is *steadiness*; the marker for gentle, accommodating, and soft-hearted types. "C" is *conscientiousness*; characterized by private, analytical, and logical.[1] I have had a lot of experience over the years giving this test and helping people understand their results. As I analyzed Jim's results I noticed that he scored very high in the "C" temperament.

I had known Jim for a number of years and didn't think this "C" matched up with who I knew him to be. He had always come off to me as a high "I." When I spoke with him, his response was, "I think that I am a high 'I.' It's just that at work I need to be much more detailed and serious in what I do. Once I get home I shift back from the 'C' mode to the 'I' mode." I asked him how he felt about that and he said, "They pay me a lot of money to be a high 'C' and I'm OK with that." But when Jim leaves his job to start his encore, he will most likely want to choose to fill his life with activities that better fit his natural behavioral style, so understanding who he really is will be very important.

Do you remember Bob and Debbie from our introduction? After ten years of living what Bob thought was the final act of his American dream, he realized that he had a lot of life left and had to figure out his road to meaning and purpose. Bob realized that he was *filling his life with fun that was increasingly not fulfilling*. So he is now on that journey to make a contribution. We would recommend to Bob that as he plans his encore he begin by taking a fresh assessment of who he is now and how his temperament is wired.

We all have come to grips with the reality that we will not be in the future what we were in the past. As we age and leave our "day jobs" and careers behind, we launch our encore with a series of new beginnings. Everything is up for grabs—location, housing, lifestyles, finances, friends, and family. What we do for meaning and purpose gets redefined. It is a fascinating question that can make us fearful. *Who do I plan to be next? What will I do for meaning and purpose, to contribute to society in these years of my life?*

Very few boomers we meet are in love with the notion of "retirement." Just ask Jay Leno. It smacks of lying on the couch and dissolving into a puddle of uselessness. We want to continue to be in the game, but we know that our roles in that game will be dramatically different. It is critical to come to the realization that you are becoming someone new in this life stage. Santiago, from *The Old Man and the Sea*, had very limited options as an old fisherman. But many of us today have a wide spectrum of possibilities for reinventing ourselves in our 60–80 Window.

Self-Assessment Tools for You

One way to find answers to these transition questions is to increase your own self-awareness. We have found it helpful at all stages of life to delve into self-assessment tools. Most of you at one time or another have probably used one or more of these tools. We would encourage you to retake one of these tests with the specific focus of identifying your current likes and dislikes, personality, how you like to do things, your wiring, and your preference in relating to people and tasks. What fuels you and what drains you? Where is your sweet spot? These tools will take you a long way toward finding your place in the 60–80 Window. Who do you want to become?

There are those in the Christian community who are a bit skeptical of these types of tools. They wonder if they are biblical, accurate from God's perspective, and reliable. Are they directly from the Bible? No. But they do reveal the patterns of our personalities, our communication style, and how we relate to people. And we believe there is a huge value to knowing these things as you go forward. As you survey the entire Bible it seems that God has a place for patterns. In nature we see the seasons of the year, the cycles of plants, and the rhythm of life as animals are born, grow up, reproduce, mature, and die.

We believe patterns found in temperament and behavior are similar to what we find in nature. God makes it clear in the Bible that we can learn scriptural principles through an analogy of the human body. We are told in 1 Corinthians 12:12 that the body is one but has many members that are different from each other. Then the apostle Paul goes on to explain:

> And if the ear should say, "Because I am not an eye, I do not belong to the body," it would not for that reason stop being

part of the body. If the whole body were an eye, where would the sense of hearing be? If the whole body were an ear, where would the sense of smell be? But in fact God has placed the parts in the body, every one of them, just as he wanted them to be. (1 Cor. 12:16–18)

Just as the body has different parts that play different roles, so we have different temperaments that make up the whole gambit of behavioral approaches to one another. As you look to what your 60–80 Window may become, we think it would be very helpful for you to take, or retake, one of the many tests available to benchmark where you are. We believe it could be beneficial to you in determining the type of things you may want to do in your encore. Some of these behaviors and preferences may have changed over the years, or will change as your lifestyle changes.

Even though I have taken all of these tests, I, Hans, took my favorite ones over again as I was in the middle of launching my encore. I found that my results in my early sixties, and with a major career shift, were quite different from what they were when I was in my forties and fifties. Many of us become what we need to be to function in a job we get paid to excel in. When our main-act career is over, we have the freedom to move toward a greater alignment between the things we do and our personalities.

In the work-a-day world there are requirements, expectations, and demands put upon us that may cause us to operate outside of our preferred temperaments, as Jim experienced. As we move into our 60–80 Window we may no longer have those demands or restraints. Therefore, retesting yourself and having a more up-to-date reading on your behavioral preferences or how you like to do things may be helpful in finding out what you will pursue in your quest for meaning and purpose in the encore part of your life.

Here is a list of and some suggestions on a few of our favorite temperament tests. These also happen to be some of the most popular ones out there today. (See the Resources section for more information on how and where you can take them.)

DiSC Assessment

We will start with the DiSC profile because we are most familiar with it. Over forty million people have taken the DiSC test.

> DiSC is a personal assessment tool used to improve work productivity, teamwork, and communication. DiSC is non-judgmental and helps people discuss their behavioral differences. If you participate in a DiSC program, you'll be asked to complete a series of questions that produce a detailed report about your personality and behavior.[2]

You need to have someone who is certified and trained to administer this test, but you can find numerous individuals and companies that will handle this for you. This test measures how you rate in four distinct temperaments: Dominance, Influence, Steadiness, and Conscientiousness. The focus is on your work behavior more than your preferences. We find it the easiest to use and remember, but other tests might be more meaningful for you.

Myers-Briggs Type Indicator

The purpose of the Myers-Briggs Type Indicator (MBTI) personality inventory is to make the theory of psychological types described by C. G. Jung understandable and useful in people's lives. The essence of the theory is that much seemingly random variation in behavior is actually quite orderly and consistent, being due to basic differences in the ways individuals prefer to use their *perception* and *judgment*.

> *Perception* involves all the ways of becoming aware of things, people, happenings, or ideas. *Judgment* involves all the ways of coming to conclusions about what has been perceived. If people differ systematically in what they perceive and in how they reach conclusions, then it is only reasonable for them to differ correspondingly in their interests, reactions, values, motivations, and skills.[3]

After taking this test you will be categorized into one of sixteen types. You end up with a four-letter combination, contrasting:

Extroversion (E) vs. Introversion (I)
Sensing (S) vs. Intuition (N)
Thinking (T) vs. Feeling (F)
Judging (J) vs. Perceiving (P)

Many people have taken the MBTI at work and used it for personal enhancement or team building with great success. I, Hans, used this first and foremost on my leadership team during my career, to give us a common language to distinguish our differences from one another. It was immensely helpful to our team, especially when conflict erupted. Donna and I also took the test together with a psychologist who helped us understand how our perception and judgment affected our marriage. We could not be more different, and that process was a huge help to our relationship. I still remember the day we sat with our psychologist friend to listen to the results.

I don't know when we have ever laughed more as a couple. We laughed and we cried because it was so very accurate and so very helpful for understanding our marriage after thirty years.

This test is more complicated than DiSC, and the complete version does require a professional to give it and interpret the results. It can be difficult to retain what the four letters stand for and how they are different from the opposing behavior, but this test is probably the most-taken instrument out there, as of our writing. We highly recommend it.

StrengthsFinder

This test has its strengths and weaknesses as well. The test is done online with a unique code found in the back of the book *StrengthsFinder 2.0*.[4] It identifies your top five strengths out of a list of thirty-four. As part of your results you get an action plan that is focused on your particular strength set and is more comprehensive than other tests. One thing we love about this test is that it is taken online and you immediately get a comprehensive document that gives you your personal assessment in writing. Everyone we know who has taken StrengthsFinder marvels at how accurate it is. This test is becoming hugely popular today and might just rank number one soon in the assessment arena.

There is no mention of areas of weaknesses, so only the positive can be addressed. In fact, the philosophy of Strengths-Finder is to focus on our strengths in our work and not focus on fixing our weaknesses. We both think that this approach is absolutely the right approach to finding convergence in our later years. Why try to fix what you are not good at? Camp on your strengths and build your encore around them.

I, Rick, want to share a great insight that I just recently gained from the value of StrengthsFinder. Recently my wife, Kathy, took the StrengthsFinder test and felt it was more helpful for her than many of the other tests. I asked her to share her thoughts on it:

> When I read the description of my five strengths that were part of my results, I found myself thinking, *How do they know this about me?* Of all of the tests I have taken, I felt this one understood me and described me most accurately. The description of each of my strengths differs from others who might have some of the same strengths because the combination of the strengths, as they relate to each other, is taken into consideration. For example, my *Maximizer* strength might look different than your *Maximizer* strength because I also have the *Achiever* strength, which you might not. I find that understanding who I am and how I function helps me to make better decisions about what to take on and what to leave to others who are better suited to the task. I feel freer to say no to opportunities that are not a good fit for me, without feeling guilty about it, and then say yes to things I know I am well equipped for. I have more joy and satisfaction in doing it, and am more successful and helpful to those I am working with.

Spiritual Gifts Assessments

Another area you might want to give some attention to is assessing your spiritual gifts. Our spiritual gifts are given to us to help us as we serve the body of Christ. These areas of gifting also carry over into our professional and personal lives.

There are a number of spiritual gift tests available online. Some have a particular theological slant, so find one that is in alignment with your particular views. Your spiritual gifts results, combined with other temperament tests, can give you a fuller perspective on who you are and what types of involvement will lead to effectiveness and fulfillment. Because of the many divergent views on this topic, we are not going to give one suggestion of an assessment tool in this category but rather encourage you to search online for one that would fit your values.

All of these assessment tools can be helpful for you in starting your journey of self-awareness. You might have a preference or want to ask others who might give you an additional perspective. I, Rick, have been doing the DiSC profile in my work and personal life for over thirty years and lean strongly toward that tool.

As you step back and try to determine what you think the future might be like for you, one of these tools can really help you in that process. Which tool you use and how involved you get with it is up to you, but this is a good starting point for entering your 60–80 Window.

18 Walking through the "Land Between"

D on't underestimate the time you will spend in the "land between." "What is that?" you ask. Just like it sounds, it is the place between the old you and the new you. It is a time of transition from the persona you were in your main career to the new person you are becoming in your encore. It is also about the transition between your life routines when you were younger to your new life situation as you age. It is about work, children, houses, friends, finances, and a host of things that change as we age. Every transition has a land between.

We are not saying you have to spend forty years there, like the children of Israel did, wandering in the desert between Egypt and the Promised Land. But there is a journey that is real and takes time. The time it takes depends on a lot of factors: your personality, your finances, your wiring, your health and mental attitude, your goals for the future, and your family situation. Each one of us is unique, so no two journeys are alike. We all have different options as we age, and those options create choices that then create transitions.

Let's call the main act of your career "point A." That is where you were camped out for many years. You raised your family there. You built a stable set of friends and life in your community and church. You probably stayed put in one place. Now things are changing and you have to figure out your "point B." We call that your encore. *There is a real emotional journey* for most people to get from point A to point B.

I, Hans, have a dear friend who was the chairman of the board at my former employer during his midseventies. He was still working full-time at his church. He was having the time of his life at age seventy-five. He retired from a career in the Target Corporation in his early sixties and then began a new career as a business administrator in his local church. And he had actually been in another career before Target. He told me he had formally retired twice, only to still be working full-time and loving every minute of it. This is another example of a rolling retirement. Today's reality is that many people will move beyond point B to C to D and maybe even to E.

We all know those days are gone when you grow up, get an education, and spend your career with one company. The days of that simple escalator ride are long over. Even if you are a professional like a doctor or lawyer, you're still going to move from place to place. And every time that move occurs there is transition. We have a good friend, an orthopedic surgeon, who recently experienced a big change in his practice when he realized he needed to sell it to make room for all the changes happening to government involvement in healthcare. He is still practicing medicine, but the stability of lifetime careers in one medical practice or law firm is over.

It takes time to process the change from A to B or B to C, though the change event itself might happen instantly. In the case of my friend Don, who was shown the door in a matter of days after a twenty-seven-year career with his company, it took him about a year in the land between to sort that all out in his heart. In other cases, like Julie Clark, whom we met in chapter 12, her transition time was almost instantaneous because her side company immediately became her new plan B. We all know friends who were abruptly shown the door after a lifelong career with one company. Their plan A was over in an instant, but it takes time to discover the ramifications, let alone discover what plan B will become. And for many of us there will also be a C and then a D as we have a rolling retirement picture.

In this period of our life stage development, we have to say goodbye to our old life role and identify and accept the new. This is an ongoing process that has actually been going on our whole life. There is no way to avoid several "land between" experiences. The quest is to move forward to the new and not get stuck in the "neutral zone"—another term for the land between. And we are not just talking about careers and jobs. There are also the transitions of many other things such as finances, friends, children, parents, marriage, health, and where we will live.

We first brought up this topic of transition in chapter 3, but it bears repeating here as we go deeper. The principles of transition can best be learned from William Bridges in his defining book *Transitions*. He describes three phases during transition.[1]

- *Endings.* The first phase of transition. You can't start a new beginning until you end your previous situation. This is the part where we leave and say goodbye to what used to be.
- *The Neutral Zone.* The second phase of transition (also known as the land between). Once you have declared

your ending you need to take some time, sit back, think, and process what it is that you are no longer a part of or what new situation you are embarking on. It may be the loss of a loved one, a job, your city and home where you lived for a long time, or your spouse. Most moms (and dads too) feel the loss of their children as the nest becomes empty as a huge transition that throws them into a prolonged neutral zone. There are a myriad of transitions that we go through and we need to actually process what it is we are transitioning from and to.

- *The New Beginning.* The third phase of the transition. You can't start a new beginning until you have completed the ending and processed getting out of the neutral zone. If you start the new beginning anywhere else it short-circuits the process. Life in the elderlescence stage is filled with many new beginnings.

Let's talk some more about this neutral zone or land between. Perhaps you are stuck there. Many people do get there and have a hard time moving forward to find those new beginnings. The neutral zone can last from a few months to several years.

Here is a dramatic story of a successful college president whose land between lasted thirteen years, which is unusually long. Everyone was stunned when Robertson McQuilkin stepped down from the presidency of Columbia International University in South Carolina to serve his ailing wife, who was suffering from Alzheimer's disease. Many would say he was in the prime of his leadership at the college. He reflected that after forty years of marriage, and his wife, Muriel, taking care of him, "I don't have to take care of her now, I get to." And so he laid aside his leadership role to care for Muriel. Both publicly and privately he said, with great joy, "She served me all these years and now is my time to serve her." He did it with great joy. He cared for her full-time for thirteen years, until her death in 2003. Then he embarked on a new career of speaking, mentoring, and writing, and eventually married a delightful woman named Debbie. His land between was a prolonged journey, and his new beginning was amazing to witness.

The land between for Robertson lasted thirteen years. How can a person who had such a fulfilling career lay it aside to become a full-time caregiver? I, Hans, remember going to their little house on Monticello Road in Columbia, South Carolina, and visiting with him and Muriel. She was bedridden and he would carefully wash her, clothe her, feed her, and read to her as he so lovingly cared for her every need. I don't think he ever anticipated that one of the greatest teachings from his life would come from this example to all of us husbands "to love our wives in sickness and in health." Robertson McQuilkin is a man who lives by vows.[2]

My father-in-law, Mark Bubeck, went through a similar experience. He was in his midseventies and already retired from being a pastor when he became the full-time caregiver to my mother-in-law, Anita. I remember being blown away when he said to me and Donna, "This is the greatest and most fulfilling ministry that God has ever called me to."

Many of us who are married will probably face the inevitable challenge of caring for our ailing spouse. We are belaboring this point to call attention to a changing reality that many of us might just face. This caregiving role might very well have to become a part of our encore.

There is a real neutral zone. Don't be afraid of it. Take time to process your transition. If you're not there yet, we are warning you to get ready for it. The worst thing to do is to live in denial. The best thing to do is to process the neutral zone with people close to you. I, Hans, am an introvert and love to process things internally. But I had to learn in my own transition to process my journey with Donna, close friends, and the TAG team we created.

So *first* of all, recognize there is a land between. *Second*, take the time to process the transition deeply in your mind and in your heart and with those close to you. *Third*—and this is so critical—you have to find the resolve to move on to your encore. If you are hesitant, you can go to that dark place and stay in your bathrobe. It's not a happy place and we don't wish it on anyone.

Getting Out of the Neutral Zone

Do you recall, when you were a kid, climbing up that long ladder to the high dive and slowing walking out to the edge and looking down? As a boy I was terrified. I am afraid of heights and it took a lot of courage for me to climb up there, and much more courage to jump off! I eventually became very good at diving, once I learned that there was no danger and that I would not die when I hit the water.

As I, Hans, went through my major career transition, I thought of this analogy of a diving board. A high dive, to be sure. When I decided to retire early and reinvent myself, I was jumping off the high dive into the great unknown.

When I sensed a strong urging in my heart of hearts that I needed to leave my old career behind and start a new beginning, I was afraid to take the plunge. I was stuck on the diving board for a long time. I would go to the edge and look down into the great unknown and back away. I was afraid to take the step. I would walk back and forth and back and forth. I would consider climbing back down the ladder.

This went on for several years! Why was I afraid? It was that same strong force that keeps so many people stuck—*fear*. I was deathly afraid of the unknown. I grew unfulfilled and bored with a job I once loved, but was too comfortable with the status quo to make a change. *Many people prefer the certainty of their misery to the misery of uncertainty.* That was me. I was stuck in the neutral zone and did not know it, because in my heart I had already emotionally left my former career.

Well, I finally jumped. And the results were a great new beginning. I have never once regretted jumping. What I do regret is that I took so long to jump . . . and wasted some good years in the neutral zone that I could have spent in my sweet spot of passion. Resolve to jump when you know in your heart of hearts that you should.

We have two acquaintances who are currently in this very place of being stuck on the board and afraid to jump. One is a woman in a high-tech job, and she hates both the job and the company's toxic culture. There is a new opportunity staring her in the face but she will not act, out of fear. Then there is an older man who has spent his career in financial services. He has plenty of money to retire and he knows he needs to leave the company. He is bored and no longer engaged, and his co-workers would really like to see him retire. But he too is paralyzed with fear. Some have defined f-e-a-r as "false expectations appearing real."

We are the lifeguards on the side of the pool watching you on the high dive, shouting, "Jump! It is safe down here and you will love it!" What does it take to jump? One word: *resolve*. Scottish explorer W. H. Murray can teach us a thing or two about resolve. In his mountain climbing expeditions, he discovered the route by which Mount Everest was eventually ascended in 1953. Murray's early life was characterized by pioneering climbing in Scotland in the 1930s, then combat against Rommel's forces during World War II in North Africa and three years in Nazi prison camps before the war finally ended. In his later years he was known as a relentless adventurer. Here is the life lesson from Murray about *resolve*, which speaks to the heart of those of us who get paralyzed by fear and fail to act. His language is a bit antiquated, but bear with us to get the meat out of what he said so many decades ago:

> This may sound too simple, but is great in consequence. *Until one is committed*, there is hesitancy, the chance to draw back, always ineffectiveness. Concerning all acts of initiative (and creation), there is one elementary truth, the ignorance of which kills countless ideas and splendid plans: *that the moment one definitely commits oneself, then providence moves too*. All sorts of things occur to help one that would never otherwise have occurred. A whole stream of events issues from the decision, raising in one's favour all manner of unforeseen incidents and meetings and material assistance, which no man could have dreamt would have come his way. I learned a deep respect for one of Goethe's couplets:
>
> > Whatever you can do or dream you can, begin it.
> > Boldness has genius, power and magic in it![3]

Get going. Begin that dream. When Murray says that "the moment one definitely commits oneself, then providence moves too," he's talking about jumping off the high dive. Be bold and providence will move to help you.

In case you're stuck in the neutral zone, let us give you some practical tips about how to move forward into your encore and get moving. For starters, jump off the board. You won't die. We promise. It doesn't do you any good to wander forever in the wilderness when there is a beautiful promised land that you can claim.

I have a great friend, Tom, who was able to retire financially in his early forties. He told me about going into the bathrobe stage of his life. He woke up late every morning and never got out of his bathrobe. He told me that the idea of retiring early is totally bogus. "That was the most miserable time of my life," he said. "I was born to be productive. I wanted to do more. I had to find something. I wandered in that wilderness for a long time before I finally decided I had to go back to work." And he proceeded to launch the encore he is now enjoying.

Action Is the Key

In the final two chapters of our book we will help you come up with an actual, concrete plan if you are not yet living your encore and need to get ready. If you are not yet there, jump right in and get started. Get committed to action. Then providence will kick in. For some of us, it will entail going back to work at a job we love. For others of us, our hobbies will become our encore career.

If you were pushed off the diving board, then process your grief about what happened to you. If you were forced out or let go before you wanted to leave, you will need to deal with your loss and the grief you might not even know you are bearing. Consider going through *The Grief Recovery Handbook* by John W. James and Russell Friedman. Get up every day, shower, shave (guys), and get dressed. Take your Wi-Fi-enabled device and go to the library or coffee shop and start looking for something you can do. Action is essential to move beyond fear and depression, out of the land between and into new beginnings.

The New Starting Line

19 Concrete Steps to Get Involved

enry David Thoreau said, "None are so old as those who have outlived enthusiasm."[1] That is a great place to start this chapter as we move into concrete action steps. Job number one is to have some enthusiasm about what lies ahead. We believe that enthusiasm about your future encore will ignite a great fire of passion within you and give you the fuel to move forward. As Pumbaa said so well in *The Lion King*, "It's times like this my buddy Timon here says: you got to put your behind in your past."[2]

Some recent research published by the Institute of Economic Affairs, a London think tank, actually proves the notion that retirement is bad for our health, stating that "Retirement has a detrimental impact on mental and physical health." In the article, "Work Longer, Live Healthier," a study by the Age Endeavour Fellowship suggests that although there is a small boost to health immediately after retirement, there is a "drastic decline in health" in the medium and long term. Retirement is found to increase the chances of suffering from clinical depression by 40 percent, while you are 60 percent more likely to suffer from a physical condition.[3]

So retirement might not be what we are pursuing, but changes will need to come. Just like Jay Leno, we have to move on to find the next thing. We all have to put our behind in our past as we look to the future. We need to discover specific ways to get engaged in new activities and roles that will bring meaning and purpose to life in the 60–80 Window. Everyone is different, and no two people or couples will take the same journey. We all have different options when it comes to the choices that lie ahead. Some people have an intense need to be very busy and accomplish things while others find much of their significance in relationships and family. There are those who long for solitude and others who need people and activity. Some in this stage are financially secure for life while others will have a great need to bring in income to make ends meet.

Both of us are high on the idea of giving back. We believe that Dr. Martin Luther King Jr. had it right when he said, "Life's most urgent question is: What are you doing for others?"[4] We believe that our encore years should be about doing things that make a contribution to our world. Sure, we should have fun, slow down a bit, and do the things we love. But we resonate with the words of Simone de Beauvoir, French philosopher and social theorist, that seem to ring so true to both of us:

> There is only one solution if old age is not to be an absurd parody of our former life, and that is to go on pursuing ends that give our existence meaning—devotion to individuals, to groups or to causes, social, political, intellectual, or creative work. . . . One's life has value so long as one attributes value to the life of others, by means of love, friendship, indignation, compassion.[5]

No matter where you find yourself, you will want to review our host of creative options to get involved, to find that meaning and purpose that you hopefully know you need. We want to explore some concrete suggestions as we share roles that are worthy to consider as options.

Options to Consider in Your Encore

Mentoring. Help those who come after us in a wide variety of roles in a workplace, church, or community. Mentoring can be with peers, those younger, and even those who are older. There is mentoring for leadership, parenting, career development, spiritual growth, marriage, and many more things than you can imagine.

Continuing to work. Keep at the job you love or find that next full- or part-time job that could use all of your life's experiences. How about being a starter at the local golf course? How about working at Trader Joe's? It is crazy for us to even begin to list all the ways you can keep working later in life. For many of us, we not only see this as an option but a necessity due to our finances. Let's try to find work in a field that really fulfills us and even gives back.

Starting another career. More than just taking the next job, try shifting to fulfilling a lifelong dream of a very different career. Hans's father went from a career in the aerospace industry to becoming a travel agent in his retirement years because he loved to travel the world.

Enjoying a rolling retirement. Dip in and out of your old career as you need to and want to. We told you the great story of Tom the firefighter, who embodies this option.

Consulting. This is a great avenue for many people in later life to capitalize on their expertise learned through a life of work.

Volunteering. There is a mother lode of opportunities in your community and your church. As with some of our other categories, it is hard to even begin a list. Go online and check out your surrounding community. Just this week our local community paper featured a big article on a new website they have set up to help people get matched with volunteering needs. If you are involved in a local church, that is a great place to start. Another concrete idea that might be useful is becoming a surrogate grandparent for children who no longer have grandparents. Not everyone has their own family later in life. In fact, increasingly, fewer people do. Some other ideas that we have seen work well are taking short-term mission trips, moving overseas for a few years, running a Christian hospitality house, helping with after-school homework assignments, tutoring children, or providing food for the homeless at your local rescue mission or food pantry.

Serving on boards. Nonprofit boards are desperate for active members and need wisdom and work in their organizations.

Intensely active grandparenting. We see some grandparents helping to raise their grandchildren. There is great joy in shaping our grandchildren's generation and pouring our values into them. Camp Grandparent is a great way to take your grandchildren on summer retreats that will greatly impact their lives.

Building a social media platform. Begin a new career on the internet where you can create a market for your products or services from the comfort of your home. This may require some ongoing education, as well as pursuing experts who can help launch this encore option with you.

Pursuing a meaningful hobby. Pour yourself into art or music or whatever brings you joy and satisfaction. We know several men who are pursuing their jazz talents and creating new bands. Then there was the lady in San Jose who discovered in her seventies that she had an amazing skill at painting. She became an accomplished artist and built a thriving business selling her artwork.

Continuing to learn. Lifelong learning keeps your mind sharp and helps you keep those faculties that you might easily lose if too much time is spent on the golf course or by the pool. Nola Ochs, the oldest known person to earn a master's degree, at age ninety-eight, went on to write a book at one hundred and certainly models this well.[6] With her example, few of us will get away with the excuse that we are just too old. Why not dig in and pursue that degree that you were always too busy to pursue, and stay engaged and inspired by signing up for a university course!

Writing. There are many ways to leave a legacy. It could be "letters to my son," where you dispense the wisdom that you have accumulated over the years, an autobiography, or anything that you feel might be a good vehicle for making a contribution to future generations. Our friend David Beavers wrote his first book in his mid-sixties called *Letters to Jonathan*, in which he talks in story format about his own life. Using fictional characters, he unveils love, joy, heartache, sorrow, the human perception of "failure," and the struggle involved in understanding redemption. David explores these on a profound level throughout his novel. What a great way to give back after a lifetime of hard-learned lessons and struggles.

Caring and caregiving. Try preparing meals, visiting lonely people in hospitals or prisons, or accompanying immigrants or older people to do some necessary paperwork. We have a friend who decided to volunteer at a local Alzheimer's care home that she drove by for years on her way to work. After retirement, she actually pulled in to the parking lot and found out that they had a desperate need for people to just come and visit with the residents.

Teaching and tutoring. Teaching English as a second language (and facing the challenge of getting a TEFL accreditation) or tutoring younger people with learning difficulties are just two ways you can pass on some of your skills and invest in younger people. Many people find that being generous with your own life carries the surprise element of receiving back far more than you had given. If your community is like most in America, it includes a steady stream of immigrants who have come to our country to seek refuge and a better life. They often feel lonely, afraid, and confused about how to make the simplest things work in their newly adopted homeland.

Relating to international students. Many foreign nationals come to America to study and then return home. While they are here they are lonely and very interested in learning more about America and our culture. We have heard it said that less than 5 percent of those international students ever get invited into an American home. What an opportunity to learn and to give to others.

Tackling a new challenge. For you to stay motivated and engaged, you might need another mountain to climb, something ahead of you that forces you to stay engaged, stretched to your limits, and feeling alive! It may be running a marathon, literally climbing a mountain, or walking "El Camino de Santiago"—something that gives you a clear focus and goal but could also be used as a fundraising opportunity where you find others to sponsor you. How about signing up to be a participant on *The Amazing Race*?

Get politically active. One way of contributing to society and shaping the future is by getting involved in politics. What political party do you subscribe to? What do they stand for? How can you be part of furthering their mandate? If you believe in what they are doing, they will want your help!

Advocacy. What are the causes that stir your passion? Whether it is advocating about protecting the lives of unborn children, political prisoners, human trafficking, climate change, religious freedom, animal rights, or the conservation of the environment—you can leave a legacy for future generations by becoming an active advocate.

Intergenerational/multigenerational engagement. It is easy to live life from a position of blame and bitterness. The young accuse the old of taking away their resources, and the old attack the young for being disrespectful and inconsiderate. One way of contributing to the well-being of the changing landscape within society is to participate and further synergetic intergenerational dialogue.

Generative Acts Give Life

Erik Erikson first wrote about "generative acts" versus stagnation in his developmental life stages that we covered in chapter 1. Webster defines *generative* as "having the power or function of generating, originating, producing, or reproducing."[7]

In a landmark study of older citizens in Australia, it was discovered that "generative acts" created a much more positive aging process than the alternative: *stagnation.* The authors took a developmental approach to successful human aging by exploring the concept of generativity in relation to older Australians' experiences of involvement in the family and community. The resulting data gives support to Erikson's contention of a generativity/stagnation crisis in later life, which we have been exploring throughout this book.

The bottom line? *Involvement in the family and community is seen as a productive and generative activity, which promotes a positive experience of aging.*[8] We all have a choice as we age: generative acts or stagnation.

The Assignment

20 Write Your Personal Encore Plan

S itting in the lobby of a hotel in Laguna Beach, we struck up a conversation with a boomer couple. They were very curious about our topic and the book you are now reading. The wife said that just the previous night, over dinner, they had been discussing their own future. They had just retired from their main careers. "We were saying to each other, 'What now?' We do not have it figured out at all, but we know that there is much more ahead for us," she said.

We have built the foundation for a plan. You know there are choices to make. Now let's finish this book with a challenge for you: to write up your plan. We know how easy it would be at this point to toss this book aside and go on to the next, but please don't, not just yet. Our deep desire is for you to put a plan down on paper. Not a perfect plan . . . there is no such thing. Just get started. Put pen to paper—or start typing.

We have a free workbook you can download and use for this exercise at www.launchyourencore.com. *Please download it as your guide to this chapter.* We want to again acknowledge the great contribution of Elke Hanssmann for most of the content of this final chapter. Be sure to read the "About Elke Hanssmann" section at the close of the book.

The idea of going back to the drawing board may be both frightening and invigorating at the same time. We are writing from the assumption that you are indeed the architect and designer of your own future, but it will require you to make a significant commitment to somewhat methodically and thoughtfully compose what your life may look like.

Tony Campolo surveyed fifty people over the age of ninety-five, asking what they would do differently if they had to live life over again.[1] The top three answers were *take more risks, reflect more,* and *invest in more things that will last beyond their lifetime.* Oliver Wendell Holmes put a different slant on the same point when he wrote, "A few can touch the magic string, and noisy fame is proud to win them: Alas for those that never sing, but die with all their music in them!"[2] What a sad obituary, to die with all our music still within us. Regrets at the end of a life do not need to be the overriding theme of your life. You can choose; you must choose. By not choosing you also choose.

So—let's get to work. Like a composer, start with a blank sheet of paper and watch the melody of your future life emerge as you work through the exercises below! Different voices will add to your song as you reflect on your life up to now. Let's start this process by exploring what those different voices have to say about us. Remember that you can download our free workbook for this chapter at www.launchyourencore .com. Do yourself a favor, go there right now and download it. Things will make so much more sense.

The Nine Stages of Your Encore Plan—Overview

Writer and anthropologist Mary Catherine Bateson asserts that

> composing a further life involves thinking about the entire process of composing a life and the way in which earlier experience connects to later. It involves looking with new eyes at what has been lived so far and making choices that show the whole process in a new light and that offer a sense of completion and fulfillment.[3]

So that you don't get overwhelmed, here is the map for the rest of this chapter:

1. Listening to the voices of your past.
2. Completing the "me at my best" exercise.
3. Identifying your temperament.
4. Facing your fears.
5. Clarifying your dreams.
6. Defining your finances.
7. Prioritizing your time commitments.
8. Brainstorming specific options.
9. Envisioning the future.

1. Listening to the Voices of Your Past

Your life-mapping exercise (and if you haven't completed this, we suggest you return to chapter 8 and do this before you proceed) will have given you a significant chunk of material to work with. In light of your past life reflections, complete the questions below to identify what it is that you specifically have to offer. If you are serious about making a plan, you must go back and start with that life map. Really. It will be fun, we promise.

What DO you have to offer?

Strengths. Anyone starting a business will begin by assessing what they bring into the new venture. What personal strengths do you bring?

For example: good listener, creative mind, relational warmth, business savvy.

Exercise: On a separate piece of paper, list a minimum of fifteen strengths (character, experience, skills) that you bring as assets into your new venture. A helpful tool for a more formalized assessment of your strengths that can complement your own brainstorming is to take a StrengthsFinder assessment. (See chapter 17 and Resources.)

Principles. What principles do you live by? How do you approach things and why?

For example: I will not give up in the face of opposition.

Exercise: List five life principles that run through your whole life.

Past mistakes. What mistakes did you make and what lessons did you learn from them that you can pass on to others? Where have you failed and what lessons have you learned from your failures that you can pass on to others? It is not wise to *dwell* on the mistakes of your past, but it is a good idea to use them as teaching points for your future.

For example: I neglected my family in pursuit of my career, and now my relationship with my children is not as close as I would like it to be.

Exercise: Think of three mistakes that you have made. What advice can you pass on to someone who might be in danger of repeating those mistakes? Write down both the mistakes and the advice!

Weaknesses. What weaknesses have limited your contribution in the past? How have you developed ways to manage those weaknesses to minimize their effect?

For example: procrastination, indecisiveness, avoidance of conflicts.

Exercise: List five weaknesses that could hinder your pursuit of your new life venture. What strategies can you employ to minimize their impact on your future?

Skills. What transferrable skills are in the toolbox of your life? What are you naturally good at? Where have you consistently seen good results from your work and contribution? What jobs do you gravitate to, and which ones do you habitually procrastinate on?

For example: problem solving, negotiating, motivating people, research skills.

Exercise: List at least ten transferrable skills that come out of your previous life experience. Once you have completed your own list, find a former colleague and a friend and ask them both to complete your list with ten skills more each.

Values. What is really important to you? How do you currently spend your time, money, and energy—and what are the underlying values your choices are serving? What makes you angry or frustrates you about others? What do you fight for?

For example: generosity, inclusiveness, equal opportunities, security, adventure.

Exercise: Elicit ten of your core values—the drivers and intrinsic motivators that determine where you put your time, energy, and money. Once you have extracted the values, translate them into behavioral choices. For example: I value adventure, therefore I choose to take opportunities to discover new territory and take risks along the way.

Character. Why do people like (or dislike) you? In what ways can people count on you? What qualities within you have been a blessing to others?

For example: Reliable, fun, honest, efficient, precise, optimistic.

Exercise: Consult three people who know you well and who you know to be honest with you. Ask them for feedback about your character and look for themes that are evident in all three results. Now you can add your own perception of your character traits.

2. Completing the "Me at My Best" Exercise

In order to extract where your best contribution could be, select five incidents in your life (it could be achievements from your work, sports, academic studies, and so forth) where you feel you were at your best. Write each incident out in detail, outlining what makes it stand out for you. What happened? What were you doing? What was happening around you? Who else was involved? Do this for each individual incident and start looking for emerging patterns. What are common factors in all five incidents? What would the context and situation need to look like to again bring together the different components that you identified?

3. Identifying Your Temperament

The importance of knowing yourself before you make big choices that will affect the next few years of your life cannot be underestimated. Are you an initiator or would you rather wait for someone else to give you direction? Do you prefer stability or embrace and welcome change? Are you energized by people or prefer solitude? There are a myriad of personality inventories that can help you find a language that describes your preferences and can serve as a natural filter system through which to consider practical options. We discussed these in detail in chapter 17. The DiSC personality profile and the Myers-Briggs type inventory are among the better-researched instruments that have provided guidance and insight for many people at life's crossroads. Take at least one of the tests available and apply what you learn about yourself to your future life composition. There are many free versions, but you will gain deeper insights by discussing your results with a trained professional who can help you maximize your insights and think through applications for you. (See our Resources section.)

4. Facing Your Fears

Nothing is stronger than the paralyzing power of fear. Most regrets we have in life can be traced back to fear—most risks never taken, most relationships never pursued, most adventures unlived. Fear, we suggest, is your biggest enemy on your journey to composing your further life. Life as we know it is coming to an end. Routines, frameworks, and structures are being taken away. Laurent Daloz observes it "can be frightening to think of dismantling it, for we imagine it to be all we have and in order to 'build fresh structures, we must reach out ahead of ourselves, and we fear the chasm below.'"[4] Fear has been a constant and familiar travel companion throughout many of our lives—unwanted and uninvited but stubbornly consistent. Nothing we have done that has had any significance has been done in the absence of fear.

Elke writes of the following journey:

> In my thirties I moved to Spain, to take a job I had co-created with my new boss, unable to even speak one word of Spanish. In my midforties I set out to study for my master's degree. In

my later forties I began a romantic relationship, having been single all my adult life. Whatever new adventures I pursued, I've always needed to take Eleanor Roosevelt's advice to heart: "If the fear doesn't go away—go and do it afraid." Fear can sabotage your future from within like nothing else. It lives subtly in your heart, posing as reality and intimidating you! The best way to combat fear is to drag it into the cold light of day, name it, and fight it. Whenever you allow fear to win, your realms of choices will shrink.

Growing older brings its own set of limitations, so allowing fear to shrink your options further would be foolish. Daloz, in his research among adults returning to higher education in mid-life, often encountered the enemy of fear. He notes that fear "is born of simple anxiety of an unknown future," blinds and paralyzes us, leads to denial and passivity in the face of anticipated losses and insecurities, yet is often unclear as to what may come instead![5] We often say that F.E.A.R. stands for "false expectations appearing real." Naming and facing your fears is a great step to disarming them. Once exposed they often lose their power, or enable you to concretely combat the worst-case scenarios fear can conjure in your mind and emotions. What are some common fears that might hold you back? What are some negative naysaying voices that drag you down?

> *For example*: I am afraid that no one will want what I am creating. The phone will not ring and the emails will stop. I am afraid that I might end up lonely once I no longer go to the office. I fear isolation, loss of significance, conflict with my spouse if I am home more, and so forth.
>
> *Exercise*: Allow your fears to surface, don't suppress them. List them, as many as you can think of. Then attack each one of them: What can you do to ensure the worst-case

scenario will not happen to you? You can today choose to move out of a victim-state where life happens to you and you are a passive, disempowered recipient! For example, if you fear ill health, what can you set in motion today to ensure good health in your next chapter? For each of the fears you identified, work through this little exercise:

- What's the fear?
- What is the worst-case scenario?
- How likely is that to happen?
- What can you do today to combat it?

5. Clarifying Your Dreams

Oliver Wendell Holmes puts it so well that we have to quote him once more: "Alas for those that never sing, but die with all their music in them." Those songs are our dreams. God has planted dreams in all of our hearts. The Bible reminds us that God will give us the desires of our hearts—and often he has been the one who has planted those dreams deep within us. What have you always dreamed of doing? Accomplishing? Disappointments in life can erode those dreams and create an obstacle to dreaming again. Courage to dream again is built when we remember the many dreams that have become a reality in our lives.

To enable yourself to dream new dreams, take a few minutes and remember some things that have materialized that started as a dream in your heart. List ten dreams that have become a reality for you that you are very proud of and satisfy you as you look back over your life.

And even if you have already answered these four questions we first listed for you in chapter 7, now is a good time to go over your answers with fresh eyes.

Current situation: What are you doing right now to fill your time? Make a list of all the things that seem to be filling your calendar. Then next to each item, on a scale of 1 to 10, put a number by the level of passion/satisfaction that you get out of that activity. One means no passion, ten means there's nothing you'd rather be doing. For example, "I take care of my grandkids every Wednesday." I have a dear friend who does that every week, and he just smiles and comes alive when he tells me about it. The first step in any assessment is to take a look at what you are doing now.

What fuels you? As you look back over your life, make a list of the things that you most enjoyed doing. They could be activities, hobbies, aspects of your profession, or anything else. What are you passionate about? What lights you up? When you do these things you sense God's pleasure. Like Eric Liddell, the famous Olympic athlete, who said, "I believe God made me for a purpose, but he also made me fast. And when I run I feel his pleasure."

What are your dreams about your future? Now let's dream about the future. What would be your dream job? Whether they paid you or not, you'd love to do this. Make a list of all the things you love to fill your calendar with. Go crazy. Fill your list with fun, passion, and satisfaction.

Now add a list of ten current dreams that you have for the next chapter of your life.

Reality check: What do others think? If you were to ask your spouse or trusted friends what they think you should do, what are things you know they would mention? We highly recommend this piece of activity as you're making decisions about your future. We do not want to set ourselves up for failure by creating the kind of expectations that could never be fulfilled. If I'm sixty years old, I'm not going to become a commercial airline pilot or a brain surgeon.

6. Defining Your Finances

While dreams matter and serve as a driving force to motivate and inspire us, there are also harsh financial realities at times. What financial obligations limit your choices? What new sources of income can you identify? What financial needs can you anticipate in the future? We discussed finances in depth in chapter 6; you might want to go back to that chapter and see those notes again.

> *Exercise*: I, Hans, and my wife, Donna, did this exercise just recently as our income picture changed dramatically. It was very useful and set our hearts at peace. Make a budget of your anticipated living costs. What will be required to cover health insurance; household costs; and financial obligations to friends, family, and organizations you are supporting? How much money will you need to live on, and what money is available to be spent on new enterprises? If you use a spreadsheet, like we did, just make three columns. The first is what income you anticipate. The second column is what you have to pay each month—"must pay." Then the third column is "want tos" if there is enough money left. Then monitor your budget each month to see how you're doing.

7. Prioritizing Your Time Commitments

How much time do you want to devote to your new ventures? How much time do you have available in light of other obligations and commitments you also want to keep? We run into many people who want to have a lot of time to play and spend with grandchildren. That is perfect. Make a concrete six-month to one-year plan with an anticipated time log for how your new life choices could be incorporated into your current life structure. When would you do these new activities? Several days a week? A few times a month? (And, of course, be sure your ideas sync with your kids, the parents of said grandkids.) Then add them to your calendar. We never get what we dream about; we get what we schedule.

8. Brainstorming Specific Options

In light of what you have identified so far, what are some concrete options that are emerging for you? If you need some help getting started, go back and look at our lists of options and generative activities in chapter 19.

- Is there a specific segment of society you want to contribute to?
- Which specific organizations, institutions, or networks are catching your attention?
- What specific skills would you like to be able to use?

9. Envisioning the Future

Clarity defines reality. Being crystal clear on the future life you want will release within you the motivation, courage, and drive to actually pursue what you know you want. However, many people struggle, and countless times we hear people say, "Argh! I'm just not the visionary type." Well, do not despair. There is a way even those who are not natural visionaries have found helpful to access some of their hopes, dreams, passions, and desires for the future.

We have already talked about dreaming about your future; now we are taking it just a bit further. Again, Elke speaks from her experience:

I vividly recall a stretch in my life when I felt I was plateauing—life was ticking along, but there was a distinct absence of excitement and even some fear of the future. Was this all there was? I sat down in a park during a work assignment in Brazil with pen and paper and started to write. In the beginning it was slow and I felt uninspired. But as I got going, my thoughts started flowing and my future began to take shape before my eyes. Even now, almost ten years later, I can feel the surge of energy and the feeling of *animo* (Spanish for *spirit*)—take courage, my heart—rushing through my body. Much of what back then was a dream has since materialized!

Letter to yourself exercise: Take a blank sheet of paper, your journal, or our worksheets and imagine that you have been fast-forwarded into the future by nine years. So, if you're sixty-one now, you are writing this on your seventieth birthday. This is a letter from your seventy-year-old self to your sixty-one-year-old self, describing in great detail what your life looks like now. Where do you live? Who is sharing your life? How are you spending your days? What has happened in between? What are your dreams for your friends and family? Where would you like to be financially when you are seventy? What do you need to consider in terms of health and fitness if you want to live your newly composed life well?

Allow yourself to dream and not to let reality interfere with your thoughts too early—let thoughts and ideas flow and write from your heart. Many of our workshop participants have been amazed at how this simple exercise helped them unlock a much clearer and vivid picture of the future, which they then felt compelled to pursue! Another interesting little statistic: the likelihood of your dreams and hopes becoming reality increases by more than 50 percent if you actually formulate and write them down, since it brings them to a level of awareness where you then become far more intentional about pursuing them. Read the letter out loud to yourself—and if you are married, to your spouse (after they have completed their own letter, of course). Discuss what you have to set in motion today to be able to live your envisioned life tomorrow! Be concrete, adding action steps, deadlines, and real commitments.

Pulling It All Together

"Setting goals is the first step in turning the invisible into the visible," according to Tony Robbins.[6] By now you will have a much clearer idea about the design of your future life, the various components you need to incorporate, what matters most, and what a meaningful outlet could look like. Hopefully you have come up with a very cool plan for your encore. Now it is time to get moving. You have planned the life, now live the plan.

Stephen Covey is the author of the bestselling book *The Seven Habits of Highly Effective People*, which has sold more than fifteen million copies around the world since it was first published in 1989. He is fond of saying, "The key is not to prioritize what's on your schedule, but to schedule your priorities."[7] In order to move from insight into action, take some concrete steps to pursue your plans.

- *Explore.* What organizations, groups, or initiatives are involved in doing something you would like to be part of? Research what the actual options for involvement for you could look like.
- *Exposure.* Get your hands dirty! Plan concrete steps to get a taste of what you consider getting involved in.

- *Evaluate*. As you try out new things, take time to reflect on your experiences. What do you like about what you are doing, and what differs from your expectations?
- *Enlist support*. Consult wise owls for feedback, along with your spouse and trusted friends.

OK, we admit, we have given you a lot of work. Take a stab at it and let us know how it goes. You can contact us and ask questions at www.launchyourencore.com. As you compose the new chapters of your future life, keep a reflective journal. Record your thoughts, feelings, and adventures as you go along. I, Hans, ended up writing over 150 pages of reflections in the year after I left my main career and transitioned into my encore!

Your new life is like a pair of unfamiliar shoes—maybe slightly uncomfortable as you start walking in them, but increasingly "yours" as you continue.

You've done it! You have arrived at composing the blueprint of your future life. Now go and do it! Carpe diem! Take courage. You can! The future belongs to those who dare to create it.

> Glory belongs to God, whose power is at work in us. By this power he can do infinitely more than we can ask or imagine. (Eph. 3:20 GW)

Conclusion

If you are growing into your later life and everything is working for you . . . great. Kudos to you if you have it all figured out. For most people, staying on autopilot in your sixties is not a wise strategy. You might just hit a brick wall, a huge drop-off, or a surprise ending not to your liking. We have tried to make it clear that we all must make choices or someone else will make them for us—and what they hand us may not be in our best interest.

Like the great boomer song from the 1960s, "People get ready, there's a train a-comin'." That train speeding down the tracks is late-life issues rapidly coming into view. Since most boomers hate the terms *seniors*, *elderly*, and *retirement*, it is time to rewrite that final act into a vibrant time of retooling, reinventing, and reinvesting in those who come after us.

Bringing everything full circle, keep these three big ideas in mind as you launch your encore. The key ingredients to a life well lived in the 60–80 Window include:

- A clear goal. Seek new meaning and purpose.
- A wise process. Make the right choices you need to make.
- The right vehicle. Reinvent yourself in your elderlescence.

Thanks for going on this journey with us. We would love to hear your thoughts, input, and questions. You can reach us anytime at www.launchyourencore.com.

About the Authors

Dr. Hans Finzel is a successful author, speaker, and trusted authority in the field of leadership. He has trained leaders on five continents. For twenty years Hans served as president and CEO of international nonprofit WorldVenture. Hans is currently president of HDLeaders and delivers a weekly leadership podcast on iTunes, *The Leadership Answer Man*. He is the author of eight books, including his bestselling *The Top Ten Mistakes Leaders Make*. His books have been translated into over twenty languages. He and his wife, Donna, reside in Colorado. Contact Hans at www.hansfinzel.com.

Dr. Rick Hicks is an author, international speaker, and consultant. He served as president of Operation Mobilization (OM) USA for fourteen years and currently serves as the leader of OM's work in North America. OM is an international ministry with over three thousand workers in over one hundred countries, focused on transforming lives and communities. Rick is the cofounder of OM's Mentoring Clinic. He spends much of his time mentoring individuals and training others to be intentional mentors. Rick and his wife, Kathy, make their home in Southern California. Contact Rick at rick.hicks@om.org.

About Elke Hanssmann

Elke Hanssmann is a self-employed coach, trainer, and consultant alongside her responsibilities in leadership and staff development globally with Operation Mobilization. Her areas of expertise include intercultural training, leadership, life direction, and transition coaching. She holds a master's degree in practical coaching and mentoring from Oxford Brookes University and a diploma in theology and intercultural studies from All Nations Christian College. Elke is passionate about helping people develop their potential and enjoys working with teams and individuals to help them become more effective and fulfilled. A certified MBTI, DiSC, and cultural mapping and navigation trainer and practitioner, she acts as a thought partner, sounding board, and travel companion for leaders around the world. Elke has helped design and deliver mentoring and coaching training for more than eight years, has traveled and worked extensively around the world, and enjoys facilitating processes that help individuals find their niche. She can be contacted at elke.hanssmann@ om.org. For more information about her coaching, training, and consultancy services, check her LinkedIn profile at http:// www.linkedin.com/pub/elke-hanssmann/32/421/777.

Resources

Our Website

www.launchyourencore.com is filled with resources, worksheets, and links to other great places to explore your encore. It is also a place to connect with the authors and find out about our seminars on Launching Your Encore.

Books We Recommend

Age Power: How the 21st Century Will Be Ruled by the New Old. Ken Dychtwald (New York: Tarcher, 2000).

The Encore Career Handbook. Marci Alboher (New York: Workman, 2012).

The Grief Recovery Handbook, 20th anniversary edition. John W. James and Russell Friedman (New York: Harper Perennial, 2009).

Life Reimagined: Discovering Your New Life Possibilities. Richard Leider and Alan Weber (San Francisco: Berrett-Koehler, 2013).

Necessary Endings: The Employees, Businesses, and Relationships That All of Us Have to Give Up in Order to Move Forward. Henry Cloud (New York: HarperCollins, 2011).

The Retirement Maze: What You Should Know Before and After You Retire. Rob Pascale, Louis H. Primavera, and Rip Roach (New York: Rowman & Littlefield, 2012).

Second-Act Careers: 50+ Ways to Profit from Your Passions During Semi-Retirement. Nancy Collamer (Berkeley: Ten Speed Press, 2013).

StrengthsFinder 2.0. Tom Rath (New York: Gallup Press, 2007).

Transitions: Making Sense out of Life's Changes, second edition. William Bridges (Cambridge: Da Capo Press, 2004).

Working Identity: Unconventional Strategies for Reinventing Your Career. Herminia Ibarra (Watertown, MA: Harvard Business Review, 2004).

Online Resources and Assessment Tools

www.aarp.org

www.capmemberbenefits.org

www.discprofile.com

www.discprofile.com/what-is-disc/overview/influence

www.encore.org

www.humanmetrics.com/cgi-win/jtypes2.asp

www.lifereimagined.org

www.strengthsfinder.com/home.aspx

About Joel Beyer and Mark Anderson (Chapter 6)

Joel Beyer is an award-winning Christian author, speaker, and advisor in the areas of financial planning, money management, and life transition support. Since 1989, Joel has developed a proven process that helps his clients to manage their financial world, pursue their goals, and live a higher quality of life. Joel lives in Ramona, California, with his wife, Cecelia, serves as an elder and board member at Calvary Chapel Ramona, and serves as membership co-chair and charitable foundation board vice president for the Rotary Club of Escondido. Joel can be reached at (760) 788-5953 or through his website at www.joelbeyer.com.

Mark A. Anderson has been practicing law in Southern California since 1981. His office is located in Escondido, California. Mr. Anderson has been conducting estate planning seminars for nearly twenty-five years. Various churches, parachurch ministries, and corporations (including Forest Home Christian Conference Center, Emmanuel Faith Community Church of Escondido, Heritage Village Retirement Center, Morgan Stanley, and Edward Jones) have sponsored the seminars and benefited from his expertise in wills, trusts, and tax law. He has addressed audiences across the country and has been the guest of numerous radio programs. In 2006, he was asked to speak at the annual conference for Operation Mobilization in Germany. In addition, he is the national planned giving director for Operation Mobilization USA. Mr. Anderson has helped thousands of individuals achieve greater security, maximize charitable giving, and be better stewards of their wealth in the most cost-effective manner possible.

Notes

Introduction

1. Paul Taylor, "Growing Old in America: Expectations vs. Reality," Pew Research Group (June 29, 2009), http://www.pewsocialtrends.org/files/2010/10/Getting-Old-in-America.pdf.
2. As quoted in Jane Pauley, "What's Your Next Move?" *AARP Magazine* (January, 2014), 57.
3. George Clooney, Brainy Quote, accessed July 21, 2014, http://www.brainyquote.com/quotes/quotes/g/georgecloo413910.html.
4. Pauley, "What's Your Next Move?" 57.
5. Max Lucado, *He Still Moves Stones* (Nashville: Thomas Nelson, 1999), 67.

Part 1 The Challenge

1. Theodore Roosevelt, Brainy Quote, accessed July 21, 2014, http://www.brainyquote.com/quotes/quotes/t/theodorero120668.html.

Chapter 1 People Get Ready

1. Adapted from Alan Chapman, "Erikson's Psychosocial Development Theory," BusinessBalls.com, accessed July 28, 2014, http://www.businessballs.com/erik_erikson_psychosocial_theory.htm.
2. Adapted from Daniel Levinson, *Seasons of a Man's Life* (New York: Ballantine Books, 1978), 49.
3. Rick Hicks, "Tribal View of Life Development," based on a concept by Ray Rood.
4. "People Get Ready," lyrics by Curtis Mayfield.

Chapter 2 I Can't Get No Respect

1. Henri J. M. Nouwen and Walter J. Gaffney, *Aging: The Fulfillment of Life* (New York: Image Books, 1976), 18.
2. Janine White, "How Gen X and Gen Y Will Change Philadelphia," *Philadelphia Magazine* (February 25, 2011), http://www.phillymag.com/articles/how-gen-x-and-gen-y-will-change-philadelphia/2.
3. Ibid., comment by Trish, April 25, 2011.
4. Rob Romasco, "Ageless Myths," *AARP Magazine* (January, 2014), 70.

Chapter 3 Transition Is Unavoidable

1. Adapted from William Bridges, *Transitions: Making Sense out of Life's Changes*, expanded and updated ed. (Cambridge: Da Capo Press, 2004).
2. Adapted from Mary L. Anderson, Jane Goodman, and Nancy Schlossberg, *Counseling Adults in Transition*, fourth ed. (New York: Springer Publishing, 2012).

Chapter 4 Beware of Going to the Dark Side

1. Bernard Baruch, as quoted in *The London Observer* (August 21, 1955).
2. Charles Spurgeon, *The Treasury of David* (Pasadena, TX: Pilgrim Publications, 1885), 67.
3. Nouwen and Gaffney, *Aging*, 29.

Chapter 5 Elderlescence

1. Sally Abrahms, "Ready for Your Second Career?" *AARP Magazine* (October–November, 2013), 24.
2. Ibid., 26.
3. Eric McWhinnie, "3 Ways Baby Boomers Are Redefining Retirement," *Wall St. Cheat Sheet* (June 16, 2013), http://www.usatoday.com/story/money/personalfinance/2013/06/15/baby-boomers-redefining-retirement/2426197/.
4. Marci Alboher, *The Encore Career Handbook: How to Make a Living and a Difference in the Second Half of Life* (New York: Workman Publishing, 2012). As quoted in Abrahms, "Ready for Your Second Career?" 26.

Part 2 The Choices

1. As quoted in Bridges, *Transitions*, 77.
2. George Bernard Shaw, *Man and Superman* (Cambridge, MA: University Press, 1903), 29.

Chapter 6 Prepare for the Choices Ahead

1. Christopher A. Borman and Patricia G. Henderson, "The Career/Longevity Connection," *Adultspan Journal* 2, no. 2 (March 2005): 22.

2. Mark Anderson and Joel Beyer, "Ten Biblical Principles That Can Change Your Life," adapted and used by permission from private unpublished notes, 2014.
3. Lewis Carroll, *Alice's Adventures in Wonderland* (London: Macmillan, 1866).
4. Henry Ford, as quoted in *The Indianapolis News* (December 11, 1922), 14.

Chapter 7 Great Expectations

1. William Bridges, *Dealing Successfully with Personal Transition* (William Bridges and Associates, 1987).
2. "Passion," Merriam Webster Dictionary online, accessed August 4, 2014, http://www.merriam-webster.com/dictionary/passion.
3. Confucius, Brainy Quote, accessed July 22, 2014, http://www.brainyquote.com/quotes/quotes/c/confucius134717.html.
4. Rihana888, "Success and Achievement in Old Age—Why You are Never Too Old to Succeed," *Socyberty Advice* (August 2, 2009), http://socyberty.com/advice/success-and-achievement-in-old-age-why-you-are-never-too-old-to-succeed-2.
5. "Chariots of Fire (1981) Quotes," IMDb, accessed August 4, 2014, http://www.imdb.com/title/tt0082158/quotes.

Chapter 8 Try a Life Map

1. Leonie Sugarman, *Life-Span Development: Frameworks, Accounts and Strategies*, second ed. (Hove, East Sussex: Psychology Press, 2001), 2.
2. Graham Lee, *Leadership Coaching: From Personal Insight to Organizational Performance* (London: Chartered Institute of Personnel and Development, 2003), 56.
3. Mihaly Csikszentmihalyi, *Beyond Boredom and Anxiety: Experiencing Flow in Work and Play*, twenty-fifth anniversary ed. (San Francisco: Jossey-Bass, 2000).
4. Richard Rohr, *Radical Grace: Daily Meditations*, ed. J. Feister (Cincinnati: Franciscan Media, 1995), 64.
5. For more information, see Frederic Hudson and Pamela McLean, *Life Launch: A Passionate Guide to the Rest of Your Life* (Washington, DC: Hudson Institute Press, 2000).
6. Carl Gustav, *Modern Man in Search of a Soul* (Abingdon, England: Routledge Press, 2001), 111.

Chapter 9 Old Dogs Can Learn New Tricks

1. Thomas Jefferson, *Thomas Jefferson: Writings*, ed. Merrill Peterson (New York: Library of America, 1984), 1249.
2. Sarah Arnquist, "What Makes Us Happy," *New York Times* (June 16, 2013).
3. Haya El Nasser, "More Americans Delay Retirement, Keep Working," *USA Today* (January 24, 2013).
4. Emily Coyle, "8 Best States for the Unemployed," *Wall St. Cheat Sheet* (June 4, 2013), http://wallstcheatsheet.com/stocks/8-best-states-for-the-unemployed.html/?a=viewall.

5. "You Are Never Too Old to Succeed in Life for Success—Age Is No Excuse," *MLM Your Way* (May 1, 2009), http://www.mlmyourway.com/success-tips/mind-set/never-too-old-for-success.

6. SilentReed, "People Who Achieved Success Later in Life," Hubpages.com, accessed July 23, 2014, http://silentreed.hubpages.com/hub/what-should-i-do-with-the-rest-of-my-life.

Part 3 The Stories

1. Jane Thayer and Peggy Thayer, *Elderescence: The Gift of Longevity* (Lanham, MD: Rowman & Littlefield, 2005), 188.

Chapter 12 A Professional Finds a Second Chance

1. Excerpts used with permission of Julie Clark; for more information about Julie visit http://julieclarkairshows.com/about-julie-clark.

Part 4 The Plan

1. Yogi Berra, "Yogisms," Yogi Berra Museum and Learning Center, accessed July 24, 2014, http://yogiberramuseum.org/just-for-fun/yogisms/.

Chapter 16 Who Does God Say That I Am?

1. Abraham Lincoln, "Abraham Lincoln Quotes," Think Exist, accessed September 4, 2014, http://en.thinkexist.com/quotation/and_in_the_end-it-s_not_the_years_in_your_life/10059.html.

2. Harriet Beecher Stowe, Brainy Quote, accessed September 4, 2014, http://www.brainyquote.com/quotes/quotes/h/harrietbee388824.html.

Chapter 17 The Toolbox

1. There are many sources for good information on the DiSC test. Here is a good summary: https://www.discprofile.com/what-is-disc/overview/influence.

2. Ibid.

3. "MBTI Basics," Myers Briggs Foundation, accessed July 24, 2014, http://www.myersbriggs.org/my-mbti-personality-type/mbti-basics.

4. Tom Rath, *StrengthsFinder 2.0* (New York: Gallup Press, 2007).

Chapter 18 Walking through the "Land Between"

1. Bridges, *Transitions*, 77.

2. Check out the full story of Robertson and Muriel McQuilkin in *A Promise Kept* (Wheaton, IL: Tyndale, 1998).

3. William H. Murray, *The Scottish Himalayan Expedition* (London: J. M. Dent & Co, 1951), 6–7. Emphasis added. Note: the couplet attributed by Murray to Goethe is actually a very loose translation of *Faust*, lines 214–30, by John Anster, 1835.

Chapter 19 The New Starting Line

1. Henry David Thoreau, Brainy Quote, accessed July 28, 2014, http://www.brainyquote.com/quotes/quotes/h/henrydavid103923.html.

2. "Quotes for Pumbaa (Character)," IMDb, accessed July 28, 2014, http://www.imdb.com/character/ch0000642/quotes.

3. Gabriel H. Sahlgren, "Work Longer, Live Healthier," Institute of Economic Affairs Discussion Paper no. 46 (London: Institute of Economic Affairs, 2013), http://www.iea.org.uk/sites/default/files/in-the-media/files/Work%20Longer,%20Live_Healthier.pdf.

4. Martin Luther King Jr., Brainy Quote, accessed September 4, 2014, http://www.brainyquote.com/quotes/quotes/m/martinluth137105.html.

5. Simone de Beauvoir, *The Coming of Age*, trans. Patrick O'Brian (New York: W. W. Norton, 1996), 540–41.

6. You can read the complete story here: "Nola Ochs, World's Oldest Masters Degree at Age 98, Now Writing a Book at 100 Years Old!" *Helping You Care* (August 4, 2012), http://www.helpingyoucare.com/21553/nola-ochs-worlds-oldest-masters-degree-at-age-98-now-writing-a-book-at-100-years-old.

7. "Generative," Merriam Webster Dictionary online, accessed July 28, 2014, http://www.merriam-webster.com/dictionary/generative.

8. Jennifer Rose Warburton, Donna McLaughlin, and Deirdre Pinsker, "Generative Acts: Family and Community Involvement of Older Australians," *International Journal of Aging and Human Development* 63, no. 2, 115–37.

Chapter 20 The Assignment

1. Tony Campolo, sermon, "If I Had to Live It Over Again," accessed July 28, 2014, http://tonycampolo.org/if-i-had-to-live-it-over-again/#.UtVBPdGYY5s.

2. Oliver Wendell Holmes, Brainy Quote, accessed July 28, 2014, http://www.brainyquote.com/quotes/quotes/o/oliverwend392895.html#KLmj7077rZz2MsqU.99.

3. Mary Catherine Bateson, *Composing a Further Life: The Age of Active Wisdom* (New York: Knopf, 2010), 9.

4. Laurent A. Daloz, *Effective Teaching and Mentoring: Realizing the Transformational Power of Adult Learning Experiences* (San Francisco: Jossey-Bass, 1986), 237.

5. Ibid., 92.

6. Tony Robbins, Brainy Quote, accessed September 4, 2014, http://www.brainyquote.com/quotes/quotes/t/tonyrobbin147791.html.

7. "7 Must Read Success Lessons from Stephen Covey," *Pick the Brain* (September 15, 2010), http://www.pickthebrain.com/blog/7-must-read-success-lessons-from-stephen-covey.

Follow Author
HANS FINZEL

HANS FINZEL is helping people
take their leadership to the next level.

Visit **HansFinzel.com** to hear his podcasts
and learn about great resources for leaders.

facebook.com/HansFinzel | @hansfinzel